Safe—

Not Sorry

by
Phyllis Schlafly

PERE MARQUETTE PRESS

P. O. Box 495   Alton, Illinois

Illustrations by Vic Vac

First Printing, December 1967

Printed in the United States of America

TABLE OF CONTENTS

Part One

1. What the Politicians Won't Tell...................... 5
2. Riots Secretly Subsidized........................... 9
3. Riots Don't Just Happen............................ 23
4. End of the Long, Hot Summer...................... 36
5. Leadership: Cringing or Courageous?...... 48

Part Two

6. TFX: The Flying Edsel............................. 72
7. The Big Payoff.................................... 85
8. The Injustice Department........................ 98
9. Leadership: Corrupt or Moral?................110

Part Three

10. Why Don't We Win in Vietnam?................122
11. Leadership: For Surrender or
    For Freedom.....................................135

Part Four

12. The Purge..146
13. Don't Leave Politics to the Politicians.........171

References...180

This book is affectionately dedicated to the thousands of wonderful women who gave me the full measure of their loyalty in May 1967—in the hope we may persuade enough American citizens to combine practical politics with the idealism which motivates our volunteer efforts to save our Republic.

Phyllis Schlafly

December 1967

chapter **I**

WHAT THE POLITICIANS WON'T TELL

On the eve of the 1968 political campaign, American voters are bracing themselves for the usual spate of windy oratory. Lyndon Johnson will put on his preacher act and tell us how much he loves "peace" and the poor. Democrat windbags will haul out their hackneyed slogan, "You never had it so good." Republican orators will repeat their warnings about fiscal insolvency which people won't believe because of U.S. prosperity.

Most Americans will say "ho hum," and switch on their favorite television program.

Yet, never before have national issues been so urgent, so personal, so terrifying.

Racial violence exploded in 110 American cities during 1967. Bloody riots have destroyed large areas as effectively as if they had been bombed by enemy planes.

Women and children in our cities live in constant fear of criminal attacks. The homes and streets of America are no longer safe. Since 1960, serious crimes have risen 62%, while the population has risen only 9%.[1]

War drags on and on and on in Vietnam—killing American boys by the thousands—with no hope of victory. Everywhere Americans ask, *Why* don't we go ahead and win it? Our nation, which could simultaneously defeat two powerful military nations on two farflung fronts (Germany and Japan in World War II), should surely be able to defeat the poor little half-country of North Vietnam in a three-year war.

What happened to the great military superiority America had when President Eisenhower left the White House in 1961? Are we really in danger of a nuclear Pearl Harbor?

The moral sickness of the Federal Government becomes more apparent every day. Public officials are caught in a giant web of payoffs, bribes, perversion, and conflicts of interest, so that few dare to speak out against the establishment.

We have a no-win war in Vietnam, a no-prosecute war on crime and Communism, and a no-work war on poverty. Is it any wonder we are not winning any of them?

Will the politicians talk frankly to American voters on these issues? You know they won't. Voters will be showered with a torrent of platitudes. Campaign orators will emote with ringing eloquence—about a lot of trivia.

The plain fact is that most* politicians haven't the courage to discuss these big issues of the 1968 campaign—the issues that affect you and the safety of your loved ones.

The Democrats cannot discuss these issues because the voters would then hold them to account for their stewardship during the last seven years.

Most liberal Republicans likewise will not discuss these big issues. They say the Democrats have been in office for 28 out of the last 36 years so we should imitate their success. Most liberal Republicans absolutely will not oppose the Democrat spending, giveaway, and soft-on-crime-and-Communism policies.

Even some mainstream Republicans avoid coming to grips with these big issues. Public relations advisers have told them to sit tight on the issue of Vietnam and not to criticize the President. They say he has too many propaganda weapons with which he can twist the Vietnam war to his own political advantage in a campaign year (as President Kennedy did with the Cuban crisis in 1962)—and the voters won't find out the truth until after the election is over.

---

*Not all, fortunately. We still have a few courageous politicians, and a few more who are courageous on *some* issues.

Candidates are simply afraid to speak out on the issue of riots and crime for fear of losing some hypothetical minority votes.

The spending power of the Federal Government has grown to such vast proportions that most politicians find it too risky—politically and financially —to hit the Administration where it hurts. They make impassioned speeches about minor issues, but they won't strike at the jugular.

There is a growing number of publications and organizations in the United States which courageously tell the truth about many issues. But, either because it is against their policy, or from lack of political expertise, they do not relate these issues to *politics*. Yet, politics is the *cause* of the major problems that confront us, and political action is their *solution*.

This is a book about the great issues of the 1968 campaign—written by one who has been on the inside of Republican politics since 1952, but who is not an officeholder, not a candidate, and has no relative on the government payroll or making money out of government contracts. Here are the facts you need to know—before it is too late—so you and your loved ones will be **safe** from the perils that confront us—**not sorry** that you failed to take the political action necessary to protect yourself.

chapter II

RIOTS SECRETLY SUBSIDIZED

In January 1967 an employee of LBJ's war-on-poverty program in St. Louis came to lecture to the senior class at the small high school where my oldest son was a student. The poverty worker arrived in casual costume: pink socks, skin-tight Levis, and a T-shirt with pink and orange horizontal stripes. In this intimate gathering, he revealed some truly startling information.

The man in the pink socks frankly described that his job was to persuade Negroes to trust the poverty workers, and then to organize them for "political action." He complained that Negroes might not normally react to oppression, and so his job was to stir them up whenever there was a case of "police brutality" so they would demonstrate and protest to City Hall.

The man in the pink socks was asked what would happen if the poverty money were cut off. He said this is "impossible." When pressed for his answer to this hypothetical question, he replied simply: "There would be riots in every major city."

In the summer of 1967, we saw the results of the "political action" stirred up by the poverty workers—racial violence in 110 American cities. From almost every city where rioting occurred in 1967, complaints were registered that poverty workers were busier agitating trouble than promoting programs of social benefit.

Thanks to the Office of Economic Opportunity (OEO),[1] the U.S. taxpayers now are subsidizing the civil turmoil that makes our cities unsafe for *both* whites and Negroes. The poverty war already stands accused in many cities of maintaining "dropout schools" which condone dishonesty, laziness, promiscuity, and general disrespect for law and order. The poverty agency has also become a device for putting on the Federal payroll jailbirds, subversives, and radicals who preach that Negro goals can only be achieved by violence. Fighting racial violence with OEO is like fighting fire with gasoline.

The Nashville "Liberation School"

On August 3, 1967, a Nashville Police Captain named John A. Sorace testified before the Senate

Judiciary Committee that the Nashville riots in April 1967 had been fomented by the Student "Nonviolent" Coordinating Committee (SNCC, pronounced Snick), which in turn was subsidized by Federal poverty money from the Office of Economic Opportunity (OEO). He testfiied that the Federal Government was subsidizing a SNCC "Liberation School" which was teaching Negro children "pure, unadulterated hatred of the white race." He said that a man named Fred Brooks, who was both the Nashville chairman of SNCC and director of the "Liberation School," and who was at the scene of the violence, had the use of a white 1967 Ford station wagon paid for by the Federal poverty agency. Sorace added: "A number of SNCC leaders who were arrested during the April riots have taught at the School."

Captain Sorace, whom *The New York Times* described as "a youthful, articulate witness," described how SNCC leaders had organized what they called "Operation Nashville," in which they taught young Negroes hatred of the white man, judo tactics, and how to manufacture the fire-bombs called Molotov cocktails. In a raid on the Nashville SNCC headquarters, police found booklets telling "how to cripple a city" and Molotov cocktails, one of which had the fingerprints of a former teacher at the "Liberation School." One of the teachers at the "Liberation School" was arrested for teaching rioters how to make gasoline bombs.[2]

Captain Sorace's testimony was corroborated by Nashville police Lieutenant Bob Hill who said that "hate of white people [is taught] over at the School. After classes start, no white people are allowed in."

This sensational testimony stirred an uproar in Washington. To deny the charges, OEO immediately flew to Washington Rev. J. Paschall Davis, the head of Nashville's poverty agency. Senator Edward Kennedy acted as a patron to Rev. Davis and tried to make the most out of his remarks.[3]

After Rev. Davis returned to Nashville, he evidently realized the seriousness of giving testimony under oath and had second thoughts about what he had said. Rev. Davis then sent a lengthy telegram to the Senate Committee admitting that his testimony on the "Liberation School" was "not exactly correct." When all the headlines had faded away, it was clear that Captain Sorace had told the truth.

Rev. Davis admitted that the poverty agency had provided the School with certain equipment including the station wagon for Fred Brooks. Rev. Davis admitted that the poverty agency was paying the rent for four women working at the "Liberation School," one of whom was a member of SNCC. He admitted that $7,700 of taxpayers' money from OEO had been authorized for the "Liberation School" since the Nashville riots, but claimed that this had not actually been paid yet.[4] Fred Brooks was scheduled to go on the payroll at $300 per month.

The only part of this story that seemed to embarrass the liberals was the fact that no whites were allowed in the classes of the "Liberation School." *That* was segregation, and that was really going too far, even for Edward Kennedy.

The truth of Captain Sorace's testimony was finally conceded by the poverty agency when it agreed not to give any *more* money to the

"Liberation School." It is quite clear that tax-payers' money would have continued to finance the "Liberation School" and the Nashville SNCC, had it not been for the Congressional investigation.

Foresight In Newark

Newark's Police Director predicted "riots and anarchy" more than six weeks before they occurred, and protested to poverty chief Sargent Shriver that Federal funds were being used to foment them. On May 25, 1967, Newark Police Director Dominick A. Spina sent a telegram to Shriver charging that OEO resources and manpower were being used "for the purpose of fomenting and agitating against the organized and democratic government and agencies" of Newark. Spina cited particularly the rental of an automobile with sound equipment which poured out inflammatory propaganda. Spina charged further that poverty workers were being "threatened with loss of their jobs if they do not participate in picketing and demonstrating."[5] Nobody denied Spina's charges.

After the bloody riots in Newark July 12-16 which claimed 27 lives, Congress began to investigate. The bipartisan investigation conducted by the House Education and Labor Committee revealed that poverty workers triggered the riot by arranging a "Police Brutality Mass Rally" in front of the police station following an insignificant incident. The riot started five minutes after the Rally began. This investigation stated that Charles McCray, the accountant for the local poverty agency, was arrested during the riots for firing a rifle from the window of a car.[6]

The report also showed that poverty workers "were in the forefront" of all protests and demonstrations that occurred in Newark during the six weeks preceding the riots. Poverty workers were also identified as spokesmen for protestors at several meetings with local officials shortly before the riots.

Leonard F. Kowalewski, president of the policemen's fraternal order in Newark, testified before the Senate Judiciary Committee[7] that poverty workers helped bring about the Newark riots by an organized hate campaign against the Newark police. He said that for the last five years, CORE (Congress of Racial Equality) has made "vicious, insidious" attacks on the Newark police, calling them "Gestapo agents and murderers who got satisfaction from brutalizing members of a minority group." Albert Black, head of the Newark Commission on Human Rights, described the police as "animals." One of the CORE leaders who was a chief leader in these attacks was Robert Curvin, who is also a director of the Newark poverty agency.

Kowalewski further testified that the Newark Legal Service financed with Federal poverty funds, had lawyers standing by during disturbances and traffic disruptions, in case anyone was arrested. He showed the Senate Committee pictures of poverty workers, side by side with known agitators, demonstrating against the Newark city hall and against a local meat market. Senator John L. McClellan commented:

> "These statements you are making indicate that Federal funds are being used to encourage, incite riots, civil disobedience, violence, and so forth."

A month before the riots, Kowalewski had sent a letter to the Mayor warning that Newark was becoming "an armed city." He pleaded for more riot guns, better helmets, and better riot-control equipment for police.

Willie Wright, a director of Newark's poverty agency, was quoted in the press as saying, "Just a six-shooter won't be enough. Get yourself a machine gun, 'cause you're gonna need it.' Every black man should buy a tank and put it in his back yard." When asked about this statement, Wright replied:

"Complete chaos will have to prevail in the streets of American cities and blood will have to flow like water before the black man will become an accepted citizen."[8]

LeRoi Jones, Negro playwright, made a speech in the city council chamber on June 27, several days before the riots, shouting that "Hiroshima and Nagasaki will look like Sunday school picnics compared to what Newark will look like when we get through with it." Jones was arrested during the riots for shooting a gun out a car window. Two loaded revolvers and 58 shells were found in the car. LeRoi Jones is another one who has been subsidized by taxpayers' money. His Black Arts Repertory Theatre in Harlem received $115,000 from HARYOU-ACT, a section of the poverty operation. When his anti-white "theatre" was raided by police, they found a cache of automatic guns, small arms, ammunition, brass knuckles and explosives.[9]

Detective William Millard of the Newark police department, a Negro, testified that poverty workers in his city "contributed" to the riot atmosphere.[10] Newark police believe that a leaflet giving instructions on how to make a Molotov cocktail was run off on a mimeograph machine in a Newark poverty office.

The mayor of Newark testified that poverty

workers "made significant contributions" to the riots, that a leftwing group known as Students for a Democratic Society controls two of the city's eight war-on-poverty areas, and that another New Left group, the Newark Community Union project, controls another.[11]

Congressman James Gardner has in his possession the record of a violence-threatening speech made before the Newark City Council by a poverty worker still on the OEO payroll who said:

"There is going to be blood running in the streets of Newark like there has never been anywhere else in America."[12]

Jersey City Mayor Thomas J. Whelan told how, while the riot was going on in Newark, H. Rap Brown was invited by a man on the poverty payroll in nearby Jersey City to speak on a program sponsored by the Council of Churches, which has a Federal OEO grant of $142,000. Brown came and told this audience: "You built the city; go out and burn it down." Mayor Whelan continued:

"I would say, this one program in Jersey City is funding and fueling and feeding people who, in my opinion, want Jersey City to erupt into a riot."[13]

The Houston Rifle Scopes

One of the strangest activities of the poverty crowd was the case of the high-powered rifle scopes ordered by the Houston office.[14]

On July 10, 1967, an order was sent from the local poverty agency to OEO in Washington for seven rifle scopes 22 inches long, equipped with standard range settings "that can be attached to any rifle." OEO approved the order and routed it through the General Services Administration office in Forth Worth, which in turn sent it to

Kelly Field Air Force Base at San Antonio. There, a civilian employee named Lester Washington ignored OEO approval and stopped the order because, "I did not think it a suitable item for this type of organization."

The press discovered the order by asking pertinent questions of the Houston Police Chief, who then commented, "I would hate to guess what they are for, but from what we have seen in the streets recently, I can imagine."

The poverty official whose name appeared on the order, George Miller, said he could not remember sending such an unusual order.

Contradictory explanations were issued by OEO. First, the Washington office of OEO hinted that the whole thing might be a hoax, even though the order was on proper stationery. Then, OEO claimed that "no requisition was honored," which was not true.

Meanwhile, the head of the Houston office said that the intention must have been to remove the lenses from the scopes and use them for microscopes. Optical experts said there is no way a telescopic sight can be converted into a microscope.

OEO then claimed that the scopes had deteriorated so that they could no longer be used for rifle sights. Word came back from San Antonio that the scopes are "in very good condition."

George Miller suddenly remembered having sent the order, asserting that he did intend to make microscopes out of telescopes (which is impossible). He issued a statement denouncing the Police Chief for allegedly "fanning the flames of hysteria" in revealing the order.

As Alice in Wonderland said, things get

"curiouser and curiouser." Other items purchased by the Houston poverty agency include a quantity of walkie-talkies and radios for monitoring police communications.

Earlier, the Houston poverty agency had aroused the indignation of local citizens because it hired two men charged with murder in connection with the rifle killing of a policeman during the riot at Texas Southern University on May 17. They were fired only after the local press raised a furor.[15]

And Elsewhere

The most famous alumnus of the poverty program is H. Rap Brown, the violent chairman of SNCC (Student "Nonviolent" Coordinating Committee). The *Washington News* revealed on August 25, 1967 that Brown was employed by the District of Columbia poverty agency from March 1965 to June 1966.

In August 1967 the top poverty agency for the District of Columbia hired at $50 a day a Black Muslim named Rufus Mayfield, who had spent eight of his 21 years in prison for a variety of offenses. Another employee of this same Federally-financed agency is Marion Barry, former head of SNCC, who had been arrested and charged with disorderly conduct while leading demonstrators onto the Capitol grounds.[16]

Buffalo City Councilman Raymond Lewandowski said that the riot in his city was preceded by threats and attempts to intimidate him by poverty workers. He told how two VISTA (Volunteers in Service to America) workers "threatened" him that there would be a race riot unless more Negro youths were given jobs. During the subsequent riots, one of these VISTA workers was arrested.

Lewandowski said that, since the Buffalo riots, VISTA workers have been "holding weekly meetings at which more than several hundred angry militant Negroes are in attendance." He described the poverty programs as:

"a well-organized conspiracy in which Buffalo's elected representatives are being subjected to threats of riot and intimidation by anti-poverty workers."[17]

Tax-paid poverty workers participated in the 1967 New York City riot. Of the 23 hoodlums arrested for looting Fifth Avenue stores, four were employees of the poverty agency.[18] New York's Mobilization for Youth, the pilot project for the Job Corps, had on its staff several members of the Communist Party.[19] Congressman Paul A. Fino of New York told the House on September 27, 1967 that a top official in the New York City poverty program, drawing a salary of $20,500 a year, is well-known as a "hard-core Communist sympathizer." Mayor John Lindsay immediately rushed to his defense.

The City Manager of Rochester, New York accused leaders of the poverty program of making statements designed "to inflame rather than to calm" racial disorders.[20]

OEO granted $700,000 to the Southwest Alabama Farmers Cooperative Association in Selma. Louisiana's Joint Legislative Committee on Un-American Activities discovered that one employee was associated with the Kremlin-financed World Youth Festival, and that another is "a prime participant in the Black Panther movement designed to overthrow the government."[21]

In Louisville, three poverty workers were arrested on August 12, 1967 and charged with sedition. Two were field organizers for the Communist-infiltrated Southern Conference Education Fund, and the other worked for Appalachian Volunteers, Inc., supported by OEO.[22] On September 14, 1967 a specially-convened Federal court freed the defendants, ruling that the Kentucky Sedition Law cannot be enforced because of the Supreme Court decision in the Steve Nelson case.[23]

Sargent Shriver's latest brainstorm for spending OEO money was to approve a $927,000 poverty grant in Chicago to put leaders of Chicago's big South Side Negro gangs on the Federal payroll at salaries of $5,000 to $7,000 a year. The idea is that they will handle job training for Negro gang members and other youth. This, in effect, gives the gang leaders new prestige, increases their influence, and proves to youth that crime does pay.[24]

A similar "gang" program for California's San Fernando Valley was scheduled to cost the taxpayers $250,000. Its director at $9,000 per year was to be James Sherman, 25-year old gang leader with a record of 14 arrests. This program has been temporarily postponed because Sherman was arrested on June 24, 1967 for holding up a liquor store.[25]

Victor Riesel, in a column entitled "Poverty Office Riddled with Revolutionaries," described how the Office of Economic Opportunity and thousands of its tiny—sometimes store-front—headquarters are loaded with literature and promoters of street action. He said:

"Some of the latter are of the New Left, the independent Maoists, the Trotskyites, the pro-Peking Progressive Labor Party youth, and even Muscovite Communist party activities. . . . When they orate in terms of the social revolution—fight city hall, smash the establishment, crack the power structure, . . . it begets violence. . . . There are minuscule movements which inject large doses of Castroitis into the teeming regions of the turbulent poor.

"In some areas of New York City, the record will show that street gangs have been subsidized by units of the poverty 'crusade.' The teenage thugs have been wooed and even provided with money and store-front headquarters. . . . There are receipted bills to prove that men identified with the Communists have been subsidized for organizing rent strike action, street movements and picketing of city hall. There are experts who say they have evidence that youth operating on the fringe of the program have distributed leaflets containing instructions for the manufacture of Molotov cocktails."[26]

Foundation Favors

In addition to poverty funds provided by U.S. taxpayers, militant extremists have another source of easy money: the large, liberal, tax-exempt foundations.

In early 1967, CORE (Congress of Racial Equality) was in a financial crisis. So CORE set up a special fund-raising committee and put Senator Robert Kennedy on it. Two weeks later, on July 13, 1967, the Ford Foundation granted CORE $175,000. Maybe it is just coincidence that the head of the Ford Foundation is McGeorge Bundy, former White House adviser to President Kennedy who has always stood very high with the Kennedys. Robert Kennedy, who put up none of the money himself, stands to reap the political benefit by pocketing Negro votes for any future campaign he may undertake.

What will the $175,000 be used for? Floyd

McKissick, national director of CORE, promptly announced that it will be used to make Cleveland a "target city" in the civil rights struggle.[27] With Ford money, the rioters will be better organized than they were in 1966 when Cleveland was the scene of bloody riots.

Meanwhile, CORE's annual Convention passed resolutions loaded with fire and brimstone, condemning the Vietnam war as a "racist and genocidal adventure" and calling for a black draft resistance campaign. Lincoln Lynch, a national CORE organizer, said in Louisiana:

"We are through clapping our hands and marching. From now on, we must be ready to kill."[28]

Had Enough?

It is time we call a spade a spade and recognize that the primary purpose of the poverty program is *political power* in the hands of the Johnson Administration, and *social revolution* in the hands of the liberal extremists. "Had Enough" was the 1946 slogan which rid our nation of the most hated of all Federal bureaus: OPA (the Office of Price Administration). The same slogan can help us abolish OEO which has already caused far more trouble than any good it has done.

We can rid our nation of this colossal fraud *if* we have leaders who will pledge to abolish it. Republicans in Congress voted against LBJ's War on Poverty bill (which set up OEO) by a majority of nearly seven to one. Since then, some of those who voted for it have seen the light. The Congressional cloakroom comment is: "When I voted for the War on Poverty, I had no idea it was going to be fought with Molotov cocktails."

chapter III

RIOTS DON'T JUST HAPPEN

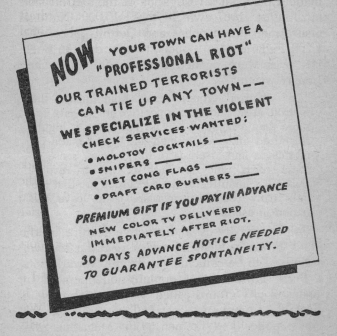

NOW YOUR TOWN CAN HAVE A "PROFESSIONAL RIOT"
OUR TRAINED TERRORISTS
CAN TIE UP ANY TOWN ─ ─
WE SPECIALIZE IN THE VIOLENT
CHECK SERVICES WANTED:
● MOLOTOV COCKTAILS ────
● SNIPERS ────
● VIET CONG FLAGS ────
● DRAFT CARD BURNERS ────
PREMIUM GIFT IF YOU PAY IN ADVANCE
NEW COLOR TV DELIVERED
IMMEDIATELY AFTER RIOT.
30 DAYS ADVANCE NOTICE NEEDED
TO GUARANTEE SPONTANEITY.

To believe that race riots are not caused by people, but by conditions such as rats and poor housing, is as silly as to believe that illegitimate babies are not caused by people but by conditions.

Riots don't "just happen"—they are organized by outside agitators and armed guerrillas, by various civil rights and New Left groups saturated with

Communists and pro-Communists, by publicity-hunters who think violence is the quickest way to glory, by professional revolutionaries filled with a hatred of Western civilization, and by Federally-financed poverty workers and assorted do-gooders who think the only way to solve the problems of the "ghetto" is to burn it down.

Louis Lomax, prominent Negro newspaperman, made a personal investigation of the Detroit riots in August 1967 which took 10,000 National Guardsmen, State police and Detroit police, plus 4,700 Federal paratroopers, several days to quell. His eyes were opened to something new, and Lomax wrote:

> "An organized group, largely from outside the Detroit area, had been operative in the city for more than a month. . . . This . . . group is highly organized and well trained and is not made up of thieves and arsonists in the ordinary sense of these words. They are, instead, causists—revolutionaries committed to the conclusion . . . that the only truly corrective measure is to leave the nation in ashes."[1]

Sniper activity is a distinctive feature of the Black Power movement, and it is all far too well organized to be coincidence. In the Newark riots, a Black Power sniper organization operated by means of city groups called "bays" which roughly resemble Communist cells.[2] They fired on hospitals, police and firemen. *Life* Magazine published interviews with the Newark snipers, who freely discussed their fraternal contact with other black extremist groups such as RAM (Revolutionary Action Movement), Deacons for Defense and Justice, and US (the Swahili-speaking group in Los Angeles). More than 50 snipers were active in the Newark riots, some of whom "had been moved in for the action from California, Ohio and Pennsylvania."[3]

After snipers had terrorized Detroit for several days, the city looked as though it had been bombed. Louis Lomax described the professional operation this way:

> "The hard core of sniper activity was highly organized. . . . Detroit's sniper activity was a precision exercise worthy of study by those who direct our troops in Vietnam. They knew the terrain, the alleys, the streets, the byways and the roof tops. They monitored police calls, set off sniper activity, and then vanished through the alleys. By midnight, Monday, they had set up a telephone squad whose job was to make false reports to the police and thus lure the officers into traps. By Tuesday, the looters and the fun seekers had their day. The professionals had taken over, and Detroit, for all practical purposes, had fallen. . . . The dedicated revolutionaries who came into Detroit and worked a brilliant military miracle were packed and gone by Wednesday."[4]

Booby-Trapping Firemen

Another distinctive aspect of the 1967 riots is the vicious attacks on firemen. None but organized criminals or Communists, determined to burn down our cities, would kill firemen trying to put out fires. Firemen were shot in the back as they climbed their ladders. Fires were often deliberately set or false alarms turned in, so that firemen could be lured into an ambush and attacked. On August 30, 1967, Albert Albertoni, secretary-treasurer of the International Association of Fire Fighters, testified before a Senate Committee on how the rioters maliciously booby-trapped buildings in order to plunge firemen into flames and burn them alive. He said:

"Floor joists are sawed part way through so that the floor will collapse when it receives the weight of the firemen who are fighting the fire. Holes have been cut in the floor near the doorway and covered with paper so that fire fighters entering the building will fall through. Stairwells have been undermined by a variety of means."[5]

During the Newark riot, 33 firemen were shot at by snipers, and three companies of firemen were "pinned in the station houses" by sniper fire. In Connecticut, Bridgeport engine house #7 was nicknamed "Fort Apache" because it was under constant attack all summer. In Cincinnati, an injured fireman was surrounded by children chanting, "Die, baby, die."[6] The 1965 Chicago riot started as an attack on firemen. In Harlem, fire engines have had to be covered with armour plate, and the tiller man on the hook-and-ladder sits in a device resembling a small steel-plated pillbox with only slits for him to look through.

Policemen, as well as firemen, are the targets of vicious, premeditated murder by the rioters. On September 27, 1967, the District Attorney of Philadelphia exposed a plot by RAM (Revolutionary Action Movement) to poison hundreds of policemen. RAM had on hand 300 grams of cyanide potassium in readiness for the next riot—at which time RAM planned to distribute the poison to various parts of Philadelphia in order to put it into coffee and sandwiches which would be given free to policemen assigned to the riot areas.[7]

Molotov cocktails are another mark of the Black Power movement. Senator Everett Dirksen revealed that a Molotov cocktail "factory" was in operation during the Detroit riot.[8] The Buffalo Police Commissioner told of a black nationalist leader, out on bail on a narcotics charge, who showed teenage boys how to make firebombs, and then urged them to break windows and loot stores, offering boys a dollar for every window they broke.[9]

Black Muslims, during the violence in Plainfield, New Jersey, organized armed squads of five men each to loot stores and ambush fire trucks.[10] An NBC television show on September 15, 1967 presented a Negro who told how he attended basement meetings in Detroit where they were instructed to break store windows, loot, and burn buildings.[11]

Maryland Governor Spiro Agnew turned over to the Justice Department a report which showed that the riots in Newark, Detroit, and Cambridge, Maryland "had a similarity in organization and execution." Inflammatory leaflets and printed instructions on how to make Molotov cocktails were circulated in all three cities prior to the outbreak of violence. Snipers were deployed in prearranged patterns and police radio broadcasts were monitored by riot organizers, who in Newark also had a walkie-talkie network.[12]

The riots prior to 1967 were organized, too. The Grand Jury report on the Cleveland riot in 1966 concluded:

> "This jury finds that the outbreak of lawlessness and disorder was both organized, precipitated and exploited by a relatively small group of trained and disciplined professionals at this business."[13]

The Carmichael-Brown Spoor

The two principal troublemakers who moved to stage-center in 1967 were Stokely Carmichael and Hubert Geroid Brown, known as H. Rap Brown. Their world is hate, violence, and riot. As they travel from city to city, they leave a spoor of moral and material destruction.

Carmichael was born in Trinidad, his mother a Panamanian. A graduate of Howard University, he has been jailed 27 times. Rap Brown was born in Baton Rouge and had three years of college. Both were rejected by the draft. As this book went to press, Carmichael was in Hanoi on a world tour of Communist capitals, and Brown was free on bond, traveling the U.S. stirring up racial violence.

Carmichael originated the slogan "Black Power" while on the James Meredith March through Mississippi in 1966. Carmichael defined Black Power at a CORE rally in Cleveland on August 6, 1966:

"When you talk Black Power, you talk of bringing this country to its knees. When you talk of Black Power, you talk of building a movement that will smash everything Western civilization has created."[14]

Carmichael was elected chairman of SNCC (Student "Nonviolent" Coordinating Committee, more properly called the Nonstudent Violent Committee) in 1966. In public appearances, he bitterly denounces the war in Vietnam and the draft. He says that Negroes are not bound to obey laws made by white people. "To hell with the laws of the United States" he often shouts to his audiences.[15] "To hell with America," he told students at Berkeley.[16]

Here are just a very few highlights of the Carmichael-Brown spoor across the United States in 1967:

April 8-10: A bloody riot erupted in Nashville, Tennessee after Carmichael and Brown had been giving speeches in the area for three days. SNCC leaders from all parts of the country had converged in Nashville for a week-long meeting just prior to the riot. Police Captain John A. Sorace later blamed the Nashville riot on Carmichael, Brown and other functionaries of SNCC, which he labelled a "black Ku Klux Klan." Sorace testified that there was every indication that the riot was "well-planned and well-organized."[17]

June 19: Rap Brown, speaking in the True Light Missionary Baptist Church in Houston, described part of his riot plan. At the outset, rioters should hit the downtown business area. There should be simultaneous outbreaks in scattered "ghettos" to split the police force. All fire hydrants should be opened. Key rioters should be dressed in regulation army uniforms which nearly match those of the guardsmen or militia so they can take over army jeeps.[18]

July 12-19: Rock-throwing, fire-bombing violence erupted in Cincinnati. Police Chief Jacob W. Schott said there had been racial harmony in Cincinnati until Carmichael and Brown urged Negroes to fight the police and burn the city. Schott added:

"I don't think we would have had trouble if these outside agitators hadn't come in and got people stirred up."[19]

July 24: Rap Brown made a "very inflammatory" speech in Cambridge, Maryland, saying:

"It's time for Cambridge to explode, baby. . . . Shoot him to death, brother, 'cause that's what he's out to do to you. Like I said in the beginning, if this town don't come 'round, this town should be burned down. It should be burned down, brother."[20]

Police Chief Brice Kinnamon later testified:

"This speech was the sole reason for our riot. . . . The street was full of guns, seconds after the speech. It was a well-organized and well-planned affair. . . . Not only did his speech cause it, but he led these people. . . . He instructed these people to shoot any patrolman, white or colored, who tried to stop them."[21]

July 26: Brown made this statement through the Washington, D.C. office of SNCC:

"We stand on the eve of a black revolution. Masses of our people are on the move."[22]

July 27: Brown told 1,000 cheering Negroes at St. Stephen's and the Incarnation Episcopal Church in Washington, D.C. that the nation is on the verge of a black revolution that will "make the Viet Cong look like Sunday school teachers." He shouted:

"Get you some guns. . . . Violence is necessary. . . . If Washington don't turn around, you should burn Washington down."[23]

August 6: Brown told a rally of 1,500 Negroes in Queens, New York that the recent racial riots were merely "dress rehearsals for revolution."[24]

August 10: Brown told a crowd of 1,000 Jacksonville, Florida Negroes:

"You've got to get yourselves some guns, brothers. I don't care if it's a BB gun with poison BBs. You better get yourselves some guns. If you are gonna loot, brother, loot a gun store. . . . Loot yourself a gun store, brother. Get yourself armed."[25]

August 18: Rap Brown called on Negroes to celebrate the anniversary of the day the Watts riots began. He explained:

"On August 18, 1965, blacks stopped moaning 'We shall overcome' and started swinging to 'Burn, baby, burn.' That was our Declaration of Independence and we signed it with Molotov cocktails and rifles."[26]

September 11: In East St. Louis, Illinois, at a rally sponsored by CORE, Brown told 1,500 Negroes:

"We need revolutionaries, not missionaries. This is the eve of a black revolution. . . . Stop singing and start swinging, chump. Get a gun."[27]

Brown then left town, having precipitated three days of vandalism, violence, fires and looting. Violent racial mobs stopped automobiles and beat the occupants. An 18-year old expectant mother was punched in the stomach while the mob yelled, "Kill that white baby; get it."[28] The vicious gang murder a month later of a 17-year old white boy was blamed by police on racial trouble stirred up by Brown.

What makes these wild Negro extremists hate America with such a passion? If they are not actually Communists, what makes them tick? Probably high on the list of motives are money and notoriety. Stokely Carmichael receives $1,500 and more for single speaking engagements. Rap Brown travels with ten bodyguards.

Malcolm X was more candid than most. He admitted that his gimmick was the statement "the white man is the devil." Malcolm X discovered that repeating this "brought me from behind prison walls and placed me on the podiums of some of the leading colleges and universities in the country."[29] What a pitiful commentary on the scholarship and standards of our colleges and universities!

Reds Behind Riots

Any lingering doubt that the Communists are behind the riots was dispelled in August 1967 when Stokely Carmichael made an illegal trip to Cuba to solemnize the alliance between his "Black Power" movement and Castro-Guevara "guerrilla warfare."

Carmichael went to attend a Communist meeting in Havana on guerrilla warfare. After listening to lengthy speeches from North Vietnamese and Viet Cong, Carmichael praised Cuba as "a shinning example of hope for our hemisphere."[30] Addressing himself to Che Guevara, the master of guerrilla warfare, Carmichael said:

> "We eagerly await your writings in order to read them, digest them, and plan our tactics based on them. . . . Do not despair, my comrade, we shall overcome."[31]

Then Carmichael issued his own call for revolution. He said that Negroes are "taking the offensive now," that "we will kill first and we will aim for the head." He called on American Negroes to "take arms and fight from New York to California, from Canada to Mexico."[32] Taking credit for the Newark riots, Carmichael said:

> "In Newark we applied war tactics of the guerrillas. We are preparing groups of urban guerrillas. . . . The price of these rebellions is a high price that one must pay. This fight is not going to be a simple street meeting. It is going to be a fight to the death."[33] The only solution to America's racial problem is "the destruction of the capitalist system, the destruction of North American imperialism. Our only possible way out is to destroy this regime or be destroyed in the attempt. In any case, we are going to fight with arms to achieve our liberation. . . . It will have to be hand-to-hand combat."[34]

The conference in Havana closed with a resolution stating that the Watts riot marked the replacement of

> "peaceful forms of protest with violent armed demonstrations against the imperialist aggression and discrimination. The path of Vietnam is our path. The continental confrontation is our path— *the creation of the second and third Vietnams in the world.*"[35] (emphasis added)

Carmichael went from Havana to Hanoi. The fact that he can travel from one Communist country to another to foment grief for the United States is visible evidence that he is able to defy our laws at will. What action did the Johnson Administration take? Only the revocation of his passport — that's all. After Carmichael returns, apparently the only restraint to be placed on him is that his illegal activities must be *confined* to the United States.

The left arm of international Communism behind the riots is RAM (Revolutionary Action Movement), oriented toward Red China, which advocates racial civil war in the U.S. RAM's "chairman-in-exile" is Robert F. Williams who fled to Cuba after shooting a policeman, and is now in Red China. RAM is racist (black men against white men), with terror as its principal weapon. Here is the way Robert Williams described RAM's objective:

"The USA will become a bedlam of confusion and chaos. The factory workers will be afraid to venture out on the streets to report to their jobs. The telephone and radio workers will be afraid to report. All transportation will grind to a complete standstill. . . . Essential pipe lines will be severed and blown up and all manner of sabotage will occur. Violence and terror will spread like a firestorm. . . . The new concept of revolution defies military science and tactics. The new concept is lightning campaigns conducted in highly sensitive urban communities. . . . The new concept creates conditions that involve the total community whether they want to be involved or not. . . . Night brings all-out warfare, organized fighting and unlimited terror. . . ."[36]

In August 1967, Williams published a 12-page folder of tips for clogging sewer lines and highways and burning public facilities without getting caught. It also advises Negro GIs to "eliminate" their white comrades in Vietnam. This folder is now being mailed from Peking to Negroes in America, and the Post Office said it is required to deliver it through the mails because of Supreme Court decisions.[37]

Phillip Abbott Luce has told how, as a Communist, he met in New York's Central Park to plan the 1964 Harlem race riots in the hope that "Harlem would herald the beginning of a nationwide guerrilla war."[38] William Epton, vice chairman of the Red-Chinese-oriented Progressive Labor Party, was indicted and later convicted of criminal anarchy for his role in these riots. In the midst of the riots, he taught people how to make Molotov cocktails. Luce concluded in his recent book:

"The record shows that the Communists will attempt to ignite riots; try to utilize an existing riot to spread violence; use a riot situation to propagandize the Negro people; and promote riots in the hope of increasing tensions between the races."[39]

The grand jury which investigated the 1966 Cleveland riots made it clear that the riots were strongly backed by Communist Party members and how the targets for fire bombing and destruction were carefully selected in advance. The report told how Communist speakers were sent in, and how extra leaders of the DuBois Clubs and the Communist Youth Party arrived in Cleveland just a few days before the riots.[40]

Red Tracks

Even without the Red words of the bosses and the hard evidence of infiltration, the depth of Communist involvement in the riots would be obvious. Just as footprints betray what kind of animal has passed our way, so Communists can be recognized by the tracks they leave.

(1) The fundamental technique of Communism is the "class war," that is, the incitement of class against class, race against race, faith against faith, management against labor, and of course Negro against white. As Herbert Aptheker, theoretician of the U.S. Communist Party, boasted: "Watts was glorious." The Communists are fundamentally "fight-promoters," and Americans should not fall for this hoary but perilous ruse.

(2) It is a mark of Communist violence that Reds kill their own in order to make "victims" to demonstrate about. In all racial violence, the ones who get hurt the most are Negroes. The Communists planned it that way. Negro lives are lost, Negro houses are burned, Negro life savings go up in smoke, Negro businesses are destroyed. The Communist purpose is not to improve but to inflame, not to heal but to cause wounds that will never lose their sting. Negro victims are deliberately killed and robbed in order to make Negroes hate the whites, hate the police, and hate America.

(3) The third mark of Red race agitation is the blackmail of middleclass Negroes. Just as the Viet Cong extort payments out of the South Vietnamese natives who want to be let alone, so middle-class Negroes are made to feel they must buy "protection" from those who are picking targets for the next riot. The violence against Negroes is coldly calculated to convince Negroes that the law cannot protect them, so they had better pay up and keep their mouths shut. This blackmail provides "sanctuaries" for extremist activities and preparations, and funds to finance arms for guerrillas.[41]

chapter **IV**

END OF THE LONG, HOT SUMMER

On August 31 and September 1, 1967 at the Palmer House in Chicago, Rev. Martin Luther King and Dr. Benjamin Spock keynoted the strangest political convention ever seen in American politics. About 3,000 revolutionaries from all over the United States assembled over Labor Day weekend for a Convention of the *National Conference for New Politics*. All the leftwing, rather-

Red-than-dead, phony-peace, draft resister, black nationalist, and racial extremist agitators gathered together under one roof for everyone to see and hear.

This Convention was a new experience for the Palmer House, one of America's most sedate and elegant hotels. The lobby, ballroom, and corridors were a seething maelstrom of dungarees, miniskirts, minks, beards, longhairs, hippies, Negroes in African attire, the Black Power cult, and even a flute player who tried to undress himself at a news conference. Hotel bedrooms were packed with as many as ten to a room. Other freakishly-dressed delegates lounged in the hallways all night. A steady stream of anti-Vietnam, Communist, and Socialist propaganda poured out of the fourth floor. One display advertised: "Revolutionary literature here — Marx, Che, Lenin, Trotsky, and Malcolm X."

Part of the Palmer House was a no-man's land from which hotel officials asked uniformed police to stay away for fear of making the violence worse than it was. Brawls were frequent and delegates (including the son of a top Communist) were robbed at knife point inside the hotel. The worst brawls were on the 11th floor where several suites had been rented by the West Side Organization, a militant Chicago civil rights group which is seeking a grant of $500,000 from LBJ's poverty agency. As the Chicago press described the Convention:

"Delegates caused more than $10,000 in damage to the Palmer House. . . . At least two marijuana parties were staged as well as several gatherings in which sex orgies were held before audiences of delegates. . . .

"While some delegates skipped out on room service and other bills, others wrote the words 'Black Power' and obscenities on the walls of hallways and rooms. . . . 'Black power' and obscenities had been carved into expensive bronze doors on virtually all of the 15 elevators in the hotel.

"At elevator entrances on various upper floors, observers reported heavy ash try urns had been smashed and the legs of tables and other furnishings broken. Elsewhere in the hotel, light fixtures on the walls of corridors had been torn free or bent. Carpeting in some rooms was gashed. . . .

"Also observed in an 11th floor room at the height of the convention was a marijuana party attended by 20 guests, who later were joined by eight naked women."[1]

In the famous children's story, Little Red Riding Hood finally got wise to the wolf in grandmother's clothing when she noticed he had such a big mouth. The NCNP Convention at the Palmer House had a mighty big mouth—and all Americans should get wise and listen. The original "call" for this Convention defined "New Politics" as "guerrilla politics," as "revolutionary politics," and as "pressure point politics, operating on society's most vulnerable points." The final "Call to Convention" boasted that this organization will "make the election process meaningful" by using "tactics of creative disorder: sit-ins and marches, rent strikes and labor strikes and school boycotts."[2]

In his speech, baby-doctor Spock urged the Convention to take "electoral action. . . . community action, and civil disobedience." He urged an immediate cease-fire in Vietnam, admission of Red China to the United Nations, and support of draft resisters. He called for "an end to the House Un-American Activities Committee and the anti-democratic, intimidating influence of the FBI."[3] Comedian Dick Gregory, in a warm-up speech, called the United States "the world's No. 1 racist country."[4]

The final resolutions passed by the Convention compared the Black Power movement to the Viet Cong guerrillas, and described the deadly riots in Newark and Detroit as "freedom wars" waged by the poor against "exploiters." The Convention also approved sending a telegram to North Vietnam and the Viet Cong expressing support for their war against South Vietnam.[5]

Black Power Blackmail

On September 1, the Convention overwhelmingly defeated a demand by the Black Power group to require 50% Negro representation on the NCNP steering committee. Instead, a resolution was passed calling for representation of *all* groups on the committee.

Black Power extremists then went into a tantrum and threatened to walk out of the Convention unless sweeping demands were met. They refused to compromise or even discuss these demands with white delegates, but gave an ultimatum that their "package" be accepted without change. These demands had been worked out in secret meetings in which only about half the Negroes were represented, and white delegates were barred altogether. The attitude of the Black Power radicals was summed up by James Forman, director of SNCC (Student "Nonviolent" Coordinating Committee), who said bluntly:

"Anyone who does not like it can go to hell."[6]

Here are some of the Black Power demands:[7]

1. Accept the concept that "there must be revolutionary change."

2. Give Negroes 50% representation on all

committees (even though Negro delegates made up only 15% of the Conference).

3. Establish "white civilizing committees" throughout the nation "to civilize and humanize the savage and beast-like character [of the whites] that runs rampant throughout America. . . ."

4. Make "immediate reparation for the historic physical, sexual, mental and economic exploitation of black people."

5. Assist local "freedom" organizations in voter registration, political education, and the election of "black candidates whom black people select."

6. Give "total and unquestionable support" to all "national people's liberation wars" in Africa, Asia, and Latin America, particularly in Vietnam, Angola, Mozambique, South Africa, and Venezuela.

7. Condemn "the imperialistic Zionist war" (apparently putting NCNP on the Arab side of the recent Arab-Israeli war).

8. Call for immediate reseating of Adam Clayton Powell and restoration to his chairmanship of the House Education and Labor Committee.

On September 2 the black extremists took over the Convention, "lock, Spock, and barrel." The big white majority capitulated to the ultimatum of the small Black Power minority and accepted *all* the above demands. Reporters covering the Convention said the Black Power advocates were astonished by their victory—they never expected their demands to be accepted.[8]

Planning "Creative Disorder"

There are a few Americans who still cling to the naive belief that there are no conspiracies and that events just spontaneously happen without anyone planning them that way. It is just as ridiculous to think that 3,000 leftists of every shade of Red and pink spontaneously converged at the Palmer House—as it is to swallow the Communist lie that 200,000 Red Chinese boys simultaneously volunteered in 1950 to cross over the Yalu River to fight American troops. Fortunately, there were some enterprising reporters who bird-dogged around the Palmer House and discovered who was masterminding the NCNP Convention.

The principal intellectual architect of this Convention was Arthur I. Waskow, formerly legislative assistant to Democrat Congressman Robert W. Kastenmeier, and now a member of the NCNP executive board. Waskow first came to public attention as one of the authors of *The Liberal Papers*, the "rather-Red-than-dead" book edited by Congressman James Roosevelt (perennial opponent of the House Committee on Un-American Activities). Waskow wrote in that revealing volume that our goal should be "the gradual dismantling of the whole [U. S.] defense organization and its replacement with an international police," and he recommended that a National Peace Agency be created to replace the Department of Defense.[9]

Waskow is now writing a book entitled *Creative Disorder*. In an article for the NCNP publication, *New Politics News*, Waskow explained what he means by "creative disorder":

> " 'Creative disorder' is intended to mean the use of techniques that are illegal, or on the edge of legality, to challenge the existing state of 'law and order' and to press toward some new kind of legal situation."

Waskow wrote that there are "five identifiable large 'movements' of people in action toward the left in America: the student movement, the Negro movement, the peace movement, the liberal-reform movement [as in the New York reform clubs and the California Democratic Council], and the religious movement [overlapping with the last two, but specifically using the churches as an organizational base]." All five "movements" were represented in the NCNP Convention.

The principal organizational talent behind the Convention was none other than the professional, experienced apparatus of the Communist Party.[10] The NCNP opened a Chicago office at 27 East Monroe Street, the same building that houses the Illinois Communist Party and the Midwest offices of the Communist *Worker*. The key Communist operating behind the scenes was Arnold Johnson, the Communist Party's national public relations director, who said at Washington University in St. Louis on May 16, 1962: "I hold a doctor of divinity degree from Union Theological Seminary. I do not believe in God."

For weeks prior to the Convention this convicted Communist was in close contact with the New York City branch office of the NCNP, and on July 29 and 30 attended the steering committee meeting in Chicago when final Convention arrangements were made.

As part of its effort to guide and control the Convention, the Communist Party issued these orders to its members:

"Attend the Convention. Become a delegate. Obtain key positions on steering committees or Convention commissions. Above all, do not allow your Communist membership to become known."[11]

Top Party boss Gus Hall gave orders that a large Red attendance was mandatory. Arnold Johnson wrote to all Party districts urging their "immediate attention" to the NCNP Convention. The Party's youth front, the W.E.B. DuBois Clubs, was assigned to work on youth delegates attending the Convention.

The NCNP was no foundling child which appeared unwanted on the doorstep of the leftwing. On the contrary, the NCNP was born in the lap of luxury at an August 1965 meeting in the multimillionaire Center for the Study of Democratic Institutions in Santa Barbara, California.[12] The chairman of the Center's Board is Supreme Court Justice William O. Douglas, perennial advocate of leftwing causes such as recognition of Red China. The Center, a wealthy offshoot of the Ford Foundation, serves principally as a gusher of tax-free foundation money to subsidize publications, meetings, and men who propagandize for nuclear disarmament and a sellout in Vietnam.[13] W. H. (Ping) Ferry, vice president of the Center, is a member of the NCNP national council.

Hidden Communist Control

Before the NCNP Convention opened, it was widely predicted that the principal result of the Palmer House meeting would be to select Martin Luther King and Dr. Benjamin Spock as "peace and freedom" candidates for President and Vice President on a new third party ticket. Preliminary soundings showed that this was favored by the majority of participating groups. Martin Luther King's announcement on August 17 that his Southern Christian Leadership Conference would "go all out to take a stand in voting for someone who is against the war in Vietnam" seemed to indicate he would throw the weight of his organization behind this effort.[14]

On the eve of the Convention, a Chicago reporter[15] disclosed that the Communist Party had plotted a different course of action. Communist Arnold Johnson persuaded the NCNP steering committee to agree on parliamentary maneuvers to prevent a Convention decision in favor of a third party campaign. Communist bosses contended that a third party effort in 1968 would be premature and futile. The Communists favor the strategy of creating and infiltrating local and precinct organizations in order to build a solid base for political action.

To the great surprise of everyone—except those who realize the power of Communist infiltration—the Convention vote was announced as 13,519 in favor of the local organizing strategy urged by the Communists, and 13,517 in favor of a third-ticket presidential campaign.[16] In other words, by this tiny two-vote margin, the Convention acquiesced in the Communist political strategy by which the radical neighborhood, youth, civil rights, and peace groups will concentrate on *local* political and organizing efforts during the coming year.[17]

Conservatives who dream of a third party ticket in 1968 should carefully study how and why the clever Communists toyed with, and then abandoned, a third party in favor of a strategy which has a far better chance of practical success.

Nobody Here But Us Chickens

The radicals have done America a big favor by staging the NCNP Convention. This put them all on display—so we can look, listen, and put up our guard. This is the way *The New York Times* summed up the delegates:

"Primarily there were opponents of the Vietnam war and militant civil rights advocates. . . . There were Communists, Trotskyites, Socialists, black nationalists, draft resisters, reform Democrats, poverty workers, refugees from Appalachia and a very few labor representatives."[18]

Here are some of the 200 groups which gathered to plot their strategy and to inflame each other's extremism.

SANE (Committee for a Sane Nuclear Policy). This propaganda organization, which promotes pulling out of Vietnam and scrapping our nuclear weapons, was represented by Dr. Benjamin Spock, the baby-doctor who can't seem to outgrow his infantile attitude toward the Soviet threat. One wag predicted that he would be the New Left's candidate for Vice President of the U.S. and would run on the slogan, "It's time for a change."

SCLC (Southern Christian Leadership Conference). Rev. Martin Luther King, chairman of this organization, was the headline attraction at the NCNP Convention.

SNCC (Student "Nonviolent" Coordinating Committee). This misnamed outfit was represented by its chairman, H. Rap Brown, who arrived at the Convention after taping a radio broadcast predicting "a great rebellion" and guerrilla warfare in all American cities. At the last minute, Brown refused to address the Convention because it was integrated; he would talk only behind closed doors to the Black Caucus of 200 Negro delegates. As Brown departed, his followers assaulted a white photographer and beat a white delegate in a hallway of the Palmer House. SNCC's former chairman, Stokely Carmichael, who has been active in NCNP since the start and is a member of NCNP's executive board, was not present, as he was in Hanoi denouncing the United States.

CORE (Congress of Racial Equality). Floyd McKissick, national director of CORE, was on hand to accept congratulations for having just received $175,000 from the Ford Foundation. In his speech to the Convention, McKissick said:

"Society has taught the black people a redefinition of violence—he who has the power to destroy has political power; he who has the power to destroy has economic power."

When a reporter asked him why he had not tried to quell the riots, he replied, "Hell, man, you made that problem. Now you clean it up."[19]

RAM (Revolutionary Action Movement). This pro-Chinese Red activist organization trains Negro guerrillas for warfare in U.S. cities and claims a Chicago membership of 200.

W.E.B. DuBois Clubs, the youth arm of the Communist Party, which J. Edgar Hoover described as "Communist-inspired, Marxist-oriented."

Local Democrat organizations. Simon Casady, former president of the California Democratic Council, was co-chairman of the Convention.[20]

Peace and Freedom Party of New York City, which ran as a candidate for Congress in 1966 Dr. Herbert Aptheker, chief theoretician of the U.S. Communist Party.

Ramparts magazine. Robert Scheer, managing editor, is a member of the NCNP steering committee. William Hinckle III, editor, has been active in NCNP since the start.

The Communist Party. Seven national leaders of the Communist Party attended as "observers," including Claude Lightfoot, chairman of the Illinois Communist Party, and Dorothy Healey, California Communist Party official.

Making Plans For 1968

All the foregoing is what the NCNP did and

said *publicly*. But that is not the whole story. When inquiring reporters interviewed the delegates privately and off the record, the Convention on New Politics turned out to be a melee of hate-mongers itching for guerrilla warfare in American cities.

Publicly, the delegates talked of "creative disorder." Privately, they made it plain that their objective is a violent, bloody revolution.

Publicly, they condemned the war in Vietnam and beat their breasts about the "terrible destruction, desolation and death." Privately, NCNP leaders expressed the hope that the war will continue indefinitely in order to force the United States to spend itself into a financial crisis which will make our country vulnerable to a Communist-led revolution.

NCNP leaders told privately how they plan to organize welfare recipients and incite them to demand ever-increasing government handouts. If the demands are met, the radicals hope this will bankrupt our nation; if the demands are rejected, this will serve as a pretext for violent insurrection.

Black Power advocates stood under the Palmer House crystal chandeliers and boasted that "Newark and Detroit were just tryouts" compared with the violence they are planning for American cities in 1968.[21]

It was mighty noisy at the Palmer House—but there was a deafening silence from the politicians. The Black Power extremists hurled the challenge —but the spineless politicians lack the courage to enforce the laws, to protect our people from guerrilla warfare, or to "insure domestic tranquillity."

chapter V

LEADERSHIP: CRINGING OR COURAGEOUS?

SIR, COULD I BRING MY WIFE TO SAIGON? - IT'S SAFER FOR HER HERE THAN IN WASHINGTON, D.C.

For 19 centuries, history has condemned Pontius Pilate who tried to wash his hands of the responsibility expected of a public official. For 19 centuries, history has condemned Nero for fiddling while Rome burned. Our voters should likewise condemn those cowardly, cringing U.S. officials who close their eyes to crime and permit our cities to burn.

Never have our people been so threatened. Never has our leadership been so lacking.

There have always been criminals in society, and there will always be. What is different about America today is that our so-called leaders are *tolerating* criminals, *negotiating* with criminals, *appeasing* criminals, *pardoning* criminals, even *subsidizing* and *rewarding* criminals. The liberal administrations have failed in a primary constitutional duty: to "insure domestic tranquillity."

Perhaps we can see a parallel in the French Revolution. Most of the supposedly substantial citizens ran away from responsibility. A determined stand by a very small number of the more substantial Frenchmen could have halted the Revolution in its tracks during the first couple of years. Mme. Roland, herself later executed, exclaimed:

> "I hope no longer that liberty may be established amongst cowards insensible to the worst outrages that could be committed against Nature and humanity, cold spectators of crimes that the courage of 50 armed men could easily have prevented."

Guerrillas in our cities can be stopped by the courage of 50 armed policemen—but not when their Mayor or their Governor forbids them to shoot.

In September 1919 a colorless, relatively unknown Governor named Calvin Coolidge suddenly faced a crisis in the domestic tranquillity of Boston. He called out the State troops with this clear statement:

> "There is no right to strike against the public safety by anybody, anywhere, at any time."

For this single act of courage, Coolidge was elected Vice President and then President of the United States.

Our country is waiting to elect as President the man who will say, "There is no right to riot (or snipe, or murder, or loot, or commit arson) against the public safety by anybody, anywhere, at any time."

No liberal can make this statement. The liberals are committed by their ideology to the absurd proposition that men do have the "right" to be criminals—if they lack an automobile, or a color TV, or if their garbage has attracted rats. The liberal clergy call this "situation ethics", which means that crime and sin are permissible depending on your situation in life. The cynical politicians just call it appealing to the minority vote.

For at least 20 years, the demagogic politicians have been in a bidding contest to win the Negro vote. They exaggerate legitimate grievances, they create grievances where none exists, and then they promise everlasting handouts in order to buy the people's vote with their own money. If you deceive people to get their money, that's fraud; but if you deceive people to get their votes, that's politics. Here are a very few samples of the way political demagogues have cruelly and extravagantly pandered to the minority vote, using language that incites to violence.

Vice President Hubert Humphrey said on July 18, 1966 in New Orleans:

"If I had to live in a slum, I think you'd have had more trouble than you've had already — because I've got enough spark left in me to lead a mighty good revolt."

Lyndon Johnson told the National Rural Electric Cooperatives in February 1959:

"I don't know how many beer bottles you folks have, but the time has come when you must ask no quarter and give none. Fight . . . in the corridors of the Capitol, in each House, generate public opinion, support your organization – and eventually, if necessary, use your beer bottles."

Senator Robert Kennedy said on August 17, 1965:

"There is no point in telling Negroes to obey the law. To many Negroes, the law is the enemy."

Governor Nelson Rockefeller on August 23, 1967 held a press conference at Expo 67 in Montreal. The Associated Press Dispatch was so sensational that we quote it here in its entirety:[1]

"*Montréal, AP* – Gov. Nelson A. Rockefeller of New York said Wednesday *racial rioting in the United States is actually a sign of progress.*

" 'There have been a lot of changes recently in the racial situation and a number of forces have been unleashed, but they're part of *the forces of progress,*' Rockefeller said during an official visit to Expo 67.

"The governor said he does not agree with a warning earlier this week by John A. McCone, former director of the Central Intelligence Agency, that the United States is in danger of being destroyed by racial strife.

" 'I'm very optimistic. The racial situation is *a sign of progress* and I believe things are improving rapidly,' Rockefeller said." (emphasis added)

Rockefeller's calling racial rioting "a sign of progress" was obviously no slip of the tongue. He said it twice, and the AP Dispatch makes it clear that he said it in the context of the bloody 1967 riots. This press conference took place just four weeks after the Detroit riots.

The Negroes are the chief victims of this type of agitation from elected public officials. After taking the politicians at their word and joining in the violence that hit 110 cities in 1967, Negroes were the ones who had to pay the bitter price.

The political agitators are still sitting in their mansions; but the rioting Negroes had their own homes and businesses burned down.

The political agitators who promise the Negroes more and more handouts are doing no favor to the Negroes. As all but the politicians now admit, the welfare program has created grave moral and social problems, such as an illegitimate birth rate of 26.32% for nonwhites,[2] and a psychology of accepting relief as a permanent way of life.

A Riot Is Like A Fire

New Jersey offers a striking contrast between the two kinds of leadership tackling the problems of crime and racial violence.

When riots erupted in Newark in July 1967, city officials hesitated. The police were given orders *not* to use their weapons. Until the riot was in its second day, Newark policemen were under orders *not* to arrest militant Negroes who were destroying property. Although 1,400 persons were arrested during the three-day Newark riot, none was arrested on the first night (July 12). City officials adopted the policy of hoping that the riots could be "contained" if the rioters were permitted to "release their pent-up emotions." Only *after* the riot was in full sway were the police permitted to "fire if necessary."[3]

In Plainfield, New Jersey, city authorities offered to pull back the troops and release some arrested Negroes in return for an effort by Negro spokesmen to cool things down. This deal with criminals did not work.

Jersey City had all the same conditions as nearby Newark—slums, race tensions, agitators financed by U.S. funds, and even Rap Brown telling Negroes to go out and burn down the town.

But Jersey City had something that made the difference between war and peace—a Mayor dedicated to doing the job he was elected for. Mayor Thomas J. Whelan, an ex-fighter pilot, immediately gave police this order:

> "Meet force with superior force, from the outset. . . . No mercy on the lawless."

Later, Mayor Whelan testified before a Senate Committee:

> "We're not prepared to hesitate one moment. When we feel this thing is under way, we're moving in with all the strength we have and we're going to crush it. . . . Both in the white and Negro communities, the people have overwhelmingly demonstrated their favor of this policy. . . . A riot is like a fire. Every fire starts with one small flame. The fire department has to get in there quickly enough with sufficient power to knock that fire out before it gets out of control."[4]

As a result of Whelan's policy of supporting his local police, Jersey City's crime rate is only 25% of what it is in New York City, and only 10% of what it is in Newark.

Detroit in July 1967 was the scene of the worst riot in the history of the United States. The toll was 43 deaths, more than $100,000,000 in property losses, 1,600 fires started, 1,700 stores looted, and 4,000 people arrested.

In Detroit the police and later the National Guardsmen were forbidden for nearly two days to use live ammunition with their weapons. They watched helplessly as looters and arsonists destroyed a large part of the city.

Negro reporter Louis Lomax told how a group of Negro ministers met with the Detroit Police Commissioner. They urged him to keep the police in check, not fire on the looters, and let looting run its course—"otherwise we would have a major riot." As a result,

> "The Detroit police instituted a maneuver that called for them to move in on the looters, chase them away, but not shoot. The result was a wild game during which the looters mocked the police for being so stupid."[5]

After the Detroit riots, a front-page story in *The New York Times* stated:

> "Many of Detroit's Negroes have turned angrily on the city's police — not for possible brutality, but for not having cracked down hard on looters when the trouble began. The Negroes say that firm action early Sunday morning when the looting began could have stopped the orgy of breaking and burning later Sunday and Monday."[6]

Detroit's Negro newspaper, *The Michigan Chronicle,* ran an 8-column banner headline reading, "It Could Have Been Stopped."

What a pitiful vacuum of leadership during the Detroit riots! While whole city blocks were in flames and snipers were terrorizing the people, while firemen were senselessly killed and families were losing their life savings, President Lyndon Johnson, Governor George Romney, and Attorney General Ramsey Clark jockeyed back and forth for political advantage. Like the irresponsible teen-agers who play the game called "chicken," each tried to see how long he could hold out before calling on the troops to restore order. Instead of protecting the white and Negro citizens of Detroit from criminal anarchy, all three played costly politics, seeking only to protect their interest in the minority vote. The Federal troops, which had been sent with speed and gusto into Little Rock, Arkansas and Oxford, Mississippi, were a tragic

two days late in Detroit. Major General Clarence
C. Schnipke, commander of the Michigan National
Guard, said on August 4, 1967:

"The problem was that the troops were not
requested by the city of Detroit until the riot
had expanded almost to its maximum intensity,
which was too late."

Milwaukee, on the other hand, gave a good
lesson in how to stop a riot. When trouble flared,
emergency plans, drafted 15 months earlier went
into action. The riot area was sealed off and an
around-the-clock curfew was imposed. Wisconsin
Guardsmen were issued live ammunition. Their
orders were, "shoot only if necessary," but "no
coddling of criminals." Looting, arson and killing
were treated as crimes. These measures sound
harsh—but they paid off. Deaths, injuries and
property losses were only a tiny fraction of what
they could have been—and of what they actually
were in Detroit and Newark.[7]

When a riot threatened in Chicago in 1966, the
Illinois National Guard was called out at once.
Commanding General Francis P. Kane immediately announced that, if the troops were fired
on, they would fire back and would "shoot to
kill." All the news media delivered this message
to the trouble spots. The result? That was the
end of the riot.[8]

"The End Of Our Dreams"

The overwhelming majority of American
Negroes are, of course, horrified and scandalized at
the riots and violence of 1967. Police Chief Schott
of Cincinnati said 95% of Cincinnati's Negroes
are "heartsick over these riots." He added:

"I know that 95% of our colored people in Cincinnati are back of the police department. They
furnish us with valuable information. But they

are afraid to speak up against this group that is
committed to violence. . . ."⁹

Yet, Negroes have been let down by their
leaders exactly as white people have been failed
by theirs. Many prominent Negro leaders have
muffed their opportunity to speak out with a loud,
clear voice for law and order. With each new
riot, a representative of CORE, or the NAACP,
blames it on the lack of Federal spending for
poverty, and predicts that riots will continue until
massive funds are channelled into the "ghettos."
As described by leading Negro newspaperman
George S. Schuyler:

> "The agitators gather crowds by blaming the
> white man for all the Negroes' ills, while the re-
> sponsible Negro leadership either defends this
> falsehood, cravenly remains silent, or whimpers
> 'we didn't really mean it' after the cities have
> burned to ashes."[10]

For example, Roy Wilkins, chairman of the
NAACP (National Association for the Advance-
ment of Colored People), blamed the race riots
on Adam Clayton Powell being deprived of his
chairmanship, on the Atomic Energy Commission
awarding the atom-smashing plant to Illinois
which does not have a fair housing law, and on
the failure of Congress to pass more civil rights
legislation. Speaking on *Meet the Press,* he added:

> "I don't consider Stokely [Carmichael] a wild one.
> I consider him the leader of the militants."[11]

Martin Luther King (whom J. Edgar Hoover
called "the most notorious liar in the country"[12])
charged on July 25, 1967 that "99%" of the racial
rioting in 1967 was "a result of inept police action."
King told the annual convention of his Southern
Christian Leadership Conference on August 15,
1967:

"I am convinced civil disobedience can curtail riots. . . . Mass civil disobedience can use rage as a constructive and creative force. . . . [Negroes] will be mentally healthier if they do not suppress rage but vent it constructively and use its energy peacefully but forcefully to cripple the operations of an oppressive society."[13]

He went on to describe his plans to "dislocate" northern cities with massive displays of civil disobedience. King listed five causes of riots, one of which is the Vietnam war.

This is not the language of a leader speaking out for law and order. This is language to inflame and incite — just a bit more delicate and more grammatical than Rap Brown's.

In vivid contrasts to Wilkins and King, there were some strong Negro voices which gave straight talk to American Negroes. Colonel David James, Jr. of Florida, a Negro pilot with 56 combat missions over North Vietnam, said from Da Nang:

Carmichael "is a big mouth who is making a profession out of being a Negro and he's got no damn business speaking for me. This Black Power garbage is for the birds. . . . When we go home, we'll have to live down the trouble he and other idiots like him have built. . . . We must speak out firmly against them and violence."[14]

Archie Moore, retired light heavyweight boxing champion of the world, gave this no-nonsense statement to the Negroes of America:

"The Devil is at work in America, and it is up to us to drive him out. Snipers and looters, white or black deserve no mercy. . . . I was born in a ghetto, but I refused to stay there. I am a Negro, and proud to be one. I am also an American, and I'm proud of that.

"The young people of today think they have a hard lot. They should have been around in the

'30s. . . . We made it because we had a goal, and we were willing to work for it. Don't talk to me of your 'guaranteed national income.' Any fool knows that this is insanity. Do we bring those who worked to get ahead down to the level of those who never gave a damn? The world owes *nobody* — black or white — a living. God helps the man who helps himself! . . .

"Granted, the Negro still has a long way to go to gain a fair shake with the white man in this country. But believe this: if we resort to lawlessness, the only thing we can hope for is civil war, untold bloodshed, and the end of our dreams."[15]

Does Poverty Cause Riots?

The liberal administrations in the White House and the State Capitols have only one solution for riots and crime—spend more taxpayers' money. One and all, they call for massive Federal spending to eliminate slums and raise the "poverty" level of the nation. The first of many big spending proposals was that Lyndon Johnson be given $1 billion for use at his discretion to help cities prevent riots. Some people seem to think any problem can be solved by enlarging the U.S. debt.

The whole idea of trying to stop riots and crime by huge Federal spending schemes is based on two false assumptions: (1) that poverty causes riots and crime, and (2) that a large percentage of Americans is hopelessly trapped in poverty.

Contrary to general belief, many rioters are not economically-deprived slum dwellers, but have jobs with medium incomes. A Detroit police detective reported:

"A good number of the guys we pulled in for looting worked steady at Ford, Chrysler and General Motors over the past three or four years. They were making $125 and $150 a week. And in some of the stores we saw looters driving off in new Cadillacs and Thunderbirds."[16]

In Highland Park, a Detroit suburb, police said 105 of 111 looters arrested had jobs and late-model automobiles.[17] Of 158 arrested in Plainfield, New Jersey, only eight were unemployed.[18]

Many riot areas are not even slums, much less "ghettos." The Cincinnati Police Chief testified that "Cincinnati does not have an area that you could describe as a 'ghetto.'"[19] Some 40% of Negro families in Detroit own their own homes.[20] The riots in Plainfield, New Jersey, and in Watts in California occurred in neighborhoods of tree-lined streets and single-family homes.

Congressman Gerald Ford said of the Grand Rapids riot in his own Michigan district:

"If there is any city in the U.S. where there was less reason for such an outbreak, I don't know it. . . . Shriver is always citing it as a model for co-operating in the poverty program."[21]

According to liberal dogma, New Haven, Connecticut should have been immune to racial violence. It was the very model of effective urban renewal and anti-poverty efforts. The Federal Government had given it the largest per capita urban renewal grant in the country—$800 for every man, woman and child in the city. Yet, New Haven erupted in the familiar pattern of looting, burning and mob action. Mayor Richard Lee said:

"I was sure that nothing like this could happen here. It just doesn't make sense."[22]

In Washington, D.C., where Negroes have the most favorable per capita income and the lowest unemployment of any city, the crime rate has increased at double the national rate. In 1967 there were 100 serious crimes every day.[23] Women cannot go down to the laundry or empty the garbage at night. There are murders even in fashionable apartment houses.[24] The State Department advises its women employees to ride the elevators in pairs and to stand near the alarm button. It is common knowledge that the State Department corridors are not safe for women after 5 P.M.[25] Earl Warren had to ask Congress for an appropriation to build a parking lot adjacent to the Supreme Court because it is not safe for the Court's women employees to walk one block to their cars at the end of the work day.[26]

LBJ has said that he is going to "extend the rule of law to outer space." He should start by extending the rule of law to our nation's capital.

Contrary to popular assumption, rioters are not necessarily "dropouts" or the poorly educated. The SNCC leadership is composed overwhelmingly of young, college-educated Negroes.[27] A study of the 1965 Watts riot revealed that one-fourth of the rioters had some college education, and many came from middleclass families with steady incomes.[28] An Urban League survey of the Detroit riots discovered:

"There was no relationship found between education and rioting. . . . Those with incomes under $2,000 . . . showed no more tendency to riot than those earning $10,000 and up."[29]

In Detroit, about half (3,595 out of 7,207) of the adults arrested in the July race riots had previous criminal records.[30] Three-fourths of those arrested during the Watts riots had police records.[31] This proves that these disorders were criminal in nature, not expressions of social protest over poverty or discrimination.

Billy Graham, in a radio broadcast in August 1967, said:

"We have been told over and over again by

some of our leaders in Washington that poverty is the cause of crime. This just is not true. . . . Poor people are not the only ones who cheat on their tax returns or commit murder. The poor do not control the national crime syndicate. The motivation for most sexual crimes is not money. People were much poorer during the Depression, and yet there was no rioting, no looting, and killing of police officers. . . . No amount of money is going to change the present situation."

Riots and crime cannot be stopped by spending vast sums of money to wipe out slums and poverty, however worthy those objectives are. If living conditions in "ghettos" were improved 1,000% tomorrow, the agitators and Communists would only say: See, we told you that riots would get you better housing, more automobiles and color TV sets; get your gun and your Molotov cocktail, and we will take over the country! Newark received the highest per capita urban renewal grants of all big cities; yet one of the Black Power leaders (described in the *Saturday Evening Post* as a "kindly-mannered, likable Negro intellectual") boasted:

"Whitey's gonna come into Newark and Detroit and the rest and try to bribe us by building a lot more public housing, and we'll burn it right down again. Where do you think those cats in the streets in Newark came out of? Right out of public housing."[32]

Liberal social theories about poverty are built on the false dogma that a "massive" number of Americans are "hopelessly trapped" in poverty. Estimates of those in poverty range from 30 million to 50 million Americans. Professor John B. Parrish, Professor of Economics at the University of Illinois, recently completely demolished the phoney statistics of the "poverty intellectuals" who make their

living out of exchanging each other's misinforma-
tion. Parrish showed that, by exaggerating poverty,
and by spawning welfare programs, the liberals
have done more to aggravate problems than to
alleviate them.[33]

Political Quackery

As a result of the urban anarchy of 1967, the
political medicine men have opened up their
bottles of quack remedies. In addition to their
principal suggestion to uncork the U.S. Treasury
for an unlimited flow of taxpayers' money to every
spending project that can be devised, there are
a variety of other suggestions to camouflage their
refusal to face reality.

On July 27, 1967, President Johnson announced
the appointment of a special Advisory Commission
on Civil Disorders, headed by Illinois Governor
Otto Kerner. The Commission is to report *in
March 1968.* This gives the Administration a fine
excuse to table any effective action now, while
the Commission meets, eats, and retreats until it
devises a wordy report telling how and why we
should spend more Federal money.

Attorney General Ramsey Clark called for
stricter gun laws. New gun laws will not stop
crime and riots any more than laws restricting
the sale of matches would stop arson. It is the
criminal who should be punished, not the gun. The
fact is that our cities may soon be like the 19th
century towns of the Western Frontier—when it
was absolutely necessary that every good guy have
his gun to protect himself and his family from
the Indians and from the villains. Nearly all the
2,700 guns stolen during the Detroit riots are
still missing.[34] It would be ridiculous, indeed, to
make it difficult for the law-abiding citizens to

have guns— while leaving the rioters in possession of their stolen guns.

Congressional liberals offered their quack remedy in the form of an anti-rat bill. Presumably it was safer to pick on rats than Reds. When the majority of the House in July 1967 refused to fall for this piece of political chicanery, 75 demonstrators from Harlem and Brooklyn shoved their way into the Capitol shouting "rats cause riots." The result? On September 20, 1967, the House reversed itself and passed the anti-rat bill. Rats are indeed a menace which needs to be controlled; but first we should note that rats of the four-legged variety have been on earth for thousands of years and have not yet caused murder, arson or looting.

Furthermore, Detroit has such an excellent rat extermination program that House Democrats, just two weeks before the bloody riots there, had cited it as a prime example of what can be done to rid a large city of rats. Detroit had "drastically reduced the incidence of rat-transmitted disease" to an average of less than one case a year in the 1960s, and no cases at all last year; and "drastically reduced the percentage of rat-infested buildings" from 9.2% of buildings checked in 1955, to less than half of 1% of buildings checked in 1966.[35]

Detroit Mayor Jerome Cavanagh called for the creation of a special 1,000-man Federal police force in each major city to fight riots. The mayor does not seem to realize that, under our system of government, the maintenance of law and order is the responsibility of local government. We do not want a national police force.

The Justice Department was busy as a beaver— *not* prosecuting the rioters—but trying to pin the blame on the newspapers that report the riots.

Officials of the Justice Department quietly met with news media in major cities to urge "restraint" in reporting racial outbursts. In other words, Americans are not supposed to know how bad guerrilla warfare already is in our country. Furthermore, the Justice Department asked the news media not to publicize the fact that these meetings took place![36] The fact is that the press has shown admirable restraint in reporting racial violence. In most cases, the damage was considerably worse than actually reported, and the tempers far more volatile.

Does Crime Pay?

The most curious quirk of the muddleheaded liberals is the way they lavish all their sympathy on the criminals—and none on their victims. We hear ad nauseam about safeguarding the constitutional rights of criminals—but nobody talks about the constitutional rights of American citizens *not* to be murdered, raped or robbed. During the last ten years, decisions of the Warren Supreme Court have made it almost as difficult to convict a criminal as it is to convict a Communist. Beginning with the infamous Mallory decision in 1957, the Warren Court has progressively tied the hands of our law enforcement officials and expanded the rights of criminals.[37]

The result of these court decisions is that the prospective criminal now believes that crime does pay. Today, the criminal knows that his chance of being convicted—and of actually serving a sentence—is so small that he can afford to take the risk. This is especially true in high-crime areas such as our nation's capital. The felon in Washington, D.C. stands only *one chance in 26* of being convicted of his crime. Despite the staggering crime rate, the D.C. prison population dropped

50% in the ten years following the Mallory decision.[38] The "anti-rat" rioters who disrupted proceedings in the Capitol on August 7, 1967 and pulled a razor on a policeman were promptly released on only $10 bail.

The court record on the Watts riots of 1965 has been a real incentive to rioters elsewhere. Of 3,927 persons arrested, only seven were sent to State prison. Jail sentences were given to 732, but nearly half of these received terms of one month or less. Only 36 received sentences of six months or more.[39]

Of the 533 arrested in Chicago's 1966 riots, only three went to State prison. On August 30, 1967, the Senate Judiciary Committee received testimony that "not a single person has been arrested and convicted [anywhere in the U.S.] because he interfered with, harassed or attacked a firefighter."[40]

One of the amazing aspects of the law enforcement problem today is the way there has been a spectacular increase in the number of pardons and sentence commutations by Lyndon Johnson in comparison with his predecessors. LBJ has opened prison doors at a rate 50% higher than the Kennedy Administration, and 100% higher than under Eisenhower. Sentence commutations are more than double the rate of the Kennedy Administration, and are 12 times the rate of the Eisenhower Administration.[41] The Federal crimes involved are sale of narcotics, tax evasion, bribery, theft of Government property, liquor violations, perjury, and transportation of obscene material. At a time when crime is higher than ever, and convictions are fewer, there is no reason to increase pardons and sentence commutations.

Justice and internal order require that punishment of criminals be prompt and certain. Justice delayed is justice denied—especially to the victims. The would-be criminal can be deterred from crime only by the knowledge that the consequences are not worth the gamble.

With law enforcement at a new low each month, with so few rioters punished, and with massive rewards in the form of new Federal handouts which follow each outbreak of racial violence, riots are bound to continue. A 1967 survey showed that 39% of Watts Negroes think the riots helped their cause.[42] Mayor Thomas J. Whelan of Jersey City described what is in store for the future:

"The establishment will continue to bestow its attention and its money on those cities which have had riots, while those cities which were able to avert disorder will be left to stand at the end of the table for whatever crumbs that are left. And thus, the degenerate bugs who hide in darkened windows and shoot down police and firemen will be rewarded and encouraged to shoot and loot again."[43]

"A Policeman's Lot Is Not A Happy One"

This famous line from Gilbert and Sullivan tells an important truth today. For a number of years, the local police have been under heavy attack from the Communists, the racial extremists, the Warren Court, and the wooly-minded liberals who want to replace law enforcement with sociology. Our present no-win war on crime has demoralized the police exactly as our no-win war in Vietnam has ruined the morale of our pilots. When we ask a man to risk his life in our behalf, he has a right to know that he has our full support.

Nearly every race riot has been touched off by a false story of "police brutality," originated by the professional agitators and then spread like wildfire. The 1967 Newark riot started with the false story that two policemen had beaten a cab driver to death. During various demonstrations, mob agitators yell, "The police are killing people," and otherwise insult the police in a deliberate attempt to aggravate the police to retaliate. "Police brutality" is a false slogan cleverly contrived to destroy some of the best and bravest Americans in our country today.

The "fallout" from decisions of the Warren Court has settled on local police departments with a vengeance. Decisions restricting the authority of police to arrest and question suspects have allowed criminals to roam the streets and have cut confessions in half.[44]

The Civilian Review Board was devised by the liberals to tie the hands of the police, to put them at the mercy of the politicians and the bureaucrats, and to remold them to conform to liberal sociology. These Boards, which have been condemned by FBI Director J. Edgar Hoover,[45] could not do otherwise but completely demoralize and frustrate the police from fulfilling their duty to maintain law and order.

The liberals are committed to the proposition that being "disadvantaged" entitles one to illegal privileges *not* enjoyed by other Americans. Permissiveness replaces morality. Police are ordered to look the other way when crimes are committed by members of a minority group. The chief victims of such lax law enforcement are the Negroes themselves, which most of them realize. Every survey taken in Negro neighborhoods (including Harlem, Cleveland, Detroit, and Watts) reveals that they want *more* police protection, not less.

The significant accomplishment of John Lindsay's term as Mayor of New York City is the demoralization of the once-great New York City police force. Fortunately, his pet project, the Civilian Review Board, which also had the backing of Governor Rockefeller, was decisively defeated in the election of November 1966. But this has not stopped Lindsay from trying to reach the same goal by other routes. New York police are made to feel that they are not supposed to make arrests if the criminals are "underprivileged" or from a minority race—even if they are caught in the act. Policemen who persist in the archaic notion that they are supposed to enforce the law are subjected to various job harassments and fail to receive promotions. The politicians, who think only about votes for the next election, exert constant pressure on police *not* to enforce the law.

Governor Nelson Rockefeller's contribution to law and order was to name a committee which produced a new New York Criminal Code. It went into effect in September 1967. At a time when the rising crime rate is a national scandal, New York now has a Code which is the most permissive, liberal and lenient in the world. The new Code itself admits:

"Changes of a fundamental nature have been wrought, upon the theory that the existing law is rooted and outmoded in 19th century theories and requires a thoroughgoing alteration of basic conceptual foundations in order to bring it into step with modern sociological, psychological and penological thinking."

It took 66 pages just to list the deletions from the old Code, that is, to name the acts which are *no longer* crimes under new sociological interpretation. No longer is it a crime in New York for a husband to abandon his pregnant wife and leave her destitute. You cannot shoot a robber making his getaway after a holdup. As a last resort, you can use a gun in self defense; but you must first give the criminal a good opportunity to kill you. You cannot use a gun against a bur-

GREAT NEWS, SARGE—YOU'VE BEEN CLEARED ON THAT CHARGE OF POLICE BRUTALITY!

glar stealing from your house or store; apparently, this is to protect the civil rights of looters.[46]

The Senate Internal Security Subcommittee Report called *A Communist Plot Against the Free World Police* clearly stated:

"Our police are among the foremost guardians of freedom and thus a major target of the Communists. The better the force, the greater its efficiency, the higher its competence in preserving the peace, the more vital it is for the Communists to destroy it."[47]

We need elected officials who will support our local police because, as retired Supreme Court Justice Charles E. Whittaker so aptly said:

"Can anyone reasonably believe that a disorderly society can survive? In all recorded history none ever has. The paths of history are strewn with the bones of fallen societies. Some of them were once as great, in many ways, as ours is now. That history also shows that, in each instance, the first evidences of the society's decay appeared in its toleration or disrespect for, and violation of, its laws."[48]

The Need For Leadership

When citizens protest the many controls exercised by an ever-growing Big Government, the favorite taunt of Great Society spokesmen is: "Just name one freedom you have lost." This challenge is now easy to answer. In the last seven years, we have lost the freedom to walk in safety on the streets of American cities. Detroit and Newark could not have occurred in the America of 1960. The riots of 1967 are the measure of how greatly crime and Communism have grown under the Johnson Administration.

The overriding reason for this tidal wave of crime is the appalling lack of courageous political leadership at the Federal, State and local levels. The cringing politicians are failing to do the job for which they were elected. They show weakness and hesitation, when they should take resolute action. They put handcuffs on the police instead of on the criminals. They fail to enforce the laws against murder, arson, theft, rape, and assault, which are crimes in every one of the 50 states. They are silent about calamitous court decisions which have crippled action against known criminals. The politicians agitate trouble and turmoil in their craven bid to buy votes with the people's own money. They succumb to the irresistible political temptation to offer tantalizing, expensive "remedies" to every problem, even though the "cure" is often worse than the disease.

It is quite possible that the racial revolutionaries will turn off their violence like a faucet during the presidential campaign of 1968—just as they turned it off after Barry Goldwater was nominated in August 1964. Americans should not again be deceived by such a temporary lull ordered for the *political* purpose of re-electing the same liberals who put us where we are today. We should remember the watchword of the Newark rioters, "You ain't seen nothing yet, baby!"

Our paramount need today is for a President, an Attorney General, Congressmen, Governors, and Mayors who have the courage to (1) accept responsibility, (2) support the police in their mission to keep order, (3) enforce the laws we already have, and (4) put forth their best efforts to correct the soft-on-crime-and-Communism court decisions, so that the constitutional rights of law-abiding citizens will again be superior to the constitutional rights of law-breakers. We need leaders such as Governor Ronald Reagan of California who, after the riots in Detroit and Newark, issued this warning to Californians:

"Those with a grievance can seek redress in the courts or legislature, but not in the streets. Lawlessness by the mob, as with the individual, will not be tolerated. We will act firmly and quickly to put down riot or insurrection wherever and whenever the situation requires."[49]

chapter VI

TFX: THE FLYING EDSEL

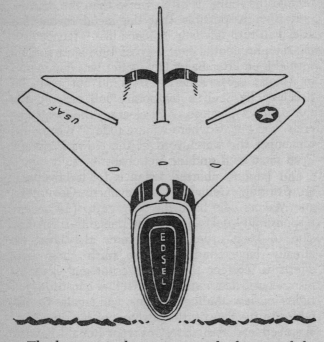

The largest single contract in the history of the United States was awarded—not to the low bidder, but to the high bidder—not for the better design, but for the poorer design—not for technical reasons, but for political reasons. This is the big story behind the famous $6.5 billion TFX contract, awarded in November 1962 to General Dynamics.

For the privilege of building 1,700 TFX fighter

planes, bids were submitted in January 1962 by two manufacturers: the Boeing Company and General Dynamics Corporation. Much suspense and anticipation built up during the many months the decision was pending, because whoever won the contract would get the choicest plum in the history of U.S. Federal spending.

Several hundred top technical Air Force and Navy experts spent 275,000 man-hours studying the competing designs. As a result, the Pentagon Source Selection Board, composed of the most experienced military experts, *unanimously* recommended the Boeing plane as better and cheaper. No evaluation group at any level ever recommended the General Dynamics plane. The Boeing plane was superior in almost every way; it had longer range and greater firepower, it could take off and land in shorter distances. The Boeing bid was $415 million lower than the General Dynamics bid.

Yet, Deputy Secretary of Defense Roswell Leavitt Gilpatric, with the approval of Secretary of Defense Robert Strange McNamara, overruled the Source Selection Board, and on November 24, 1962 awarded the contract to General Dynamics.

This announcement precipitated a storm of protest in Washington. In order to answer the criticism, Secretary McNamara, Secretary of the Navy Fred Korth, and Secretary of the Air Force Eugene Zuckert released a "Memorandum for the Record" attempting to explain why they overruled the Source Selection Board and all technical experts.[1] Here are the principal reasons this trio presented:

1. "Commonality." This was a McNamara-manufactured expression by which he claimed that "85% of the parts in the General Dynamics

version are identical, contrasted with 60% in the Boeing proposal."

2. The General Dynamics proposal "offers the better possibility of obtaining the aircraft desired on schedule and within the dollars programmed."

3. "Excessive optimism in the Boeing proposal —the apparent belief that thrust reversers can be developed . . .; the view that the variable sweep wing can be quite easily applied to the TFX concept; the use of titanium in structural members; and the unique design for the propulsion installation."

4. "In the raw score comparison, General Dynamics received 175.6 points and Boeing 172.1."

"It's All Poppycock"

McNamara's arguments were all easily refuted by aircraft experts.

1. The Navy's top civilian aeronautical engineer, George Spangenberg, testified concerning McNamara's "commonality" argument:

> "It's all poppycock. We think Boeing gave us a better proposal at a better price. You certainly don't want to pay more money to get an inferior product just because it meets some word — commonality — better."[2]

The Chairman of the Source Selection Board, General Robert Ruegg, testified that "commonality" was a liability, not an asset. He said that too much "commonality" made the Navy version too heavy to operate off a carrier.[3] Years later, after this prediction had proved absolutely accurate, McNamara's smart-alecky retort was to say that the Navy would just have to build stronger decks on the carriers.

2. McNamara's argument that General Dynam-

ics would be "on schedule and within the dollars programmed" was false when he made it. On the basis of past performance, Boeing had a better record of producing military planes within its bids than General Dynamics. Boeing had built the C-97, B-47, KC-135, and B-52 at an average of 1.1% *under* its bids. General Dynamics had built the F-102, F-106, and B-58 at an average of 4.8% *over* its bids.[4] Since the TFX contract was awarded, McNamara's argument has been proved completely ridiculous. General Dynamics is now two years behind schedule, and the cost has climbed from $2.9 million per plane to more than $8 million per plane.

3. Technical experts at the time demolished all McNamara's arguments about Boeing's "excessive optimism," and technological progress since then has proved that Boeing's "optimism" was completely valid. The Air Force Vice Chief of Staff, General William McKee, testified that the Boeing "thrust reverser" was an advantage because it "provides far better deceleration" in combat maneuvering.[5] The Boeing variable sweep-wing concept was copied by General Dynamics, and also by the Russians.[6] Engineers and metallurgists testified that titanium had already been used successfully in aircraft structural members; since then it has been even more widely used because it is so light and strong.

4. It finally came out that McNamara, supposedly such a whiz with figures, was just plain wrong in his arithmetic. In his "Memorandum for the Record" there were separate arithmetic errors of $32 million and $29 million.[7] Secretary Zuckert admitted that the "Memorandum" had falsely taken the superior Boeing performance figures and assigned them to General Dynamics. Colonel

Gayle of the Air Force said that all errors in the "Memorandum" favored General Dynamics.[8]

McNamara's defense of General Dynamics was so unsatisfactory that on February 26, 1963 a Senate investigation was begun under the chairmanship of Senator John L. McClellan. At this point, a Pentagon attorney approached Air Force Chief General Curtis LeMay and Chief of Naval Operations Admiral George W. Anderson and asked them to request Senator McClellan to drop the TFX investigation. Both men declined to do this.[9]

As witness after witness was called, it became shockingly clear that everyone with any technical credentials favored the Boeing plane, and practically no one wanted the General Dynamics plane except McNamara, Gilpatric and Korth. General LeMay testified that he could not recall a single instance where the Source Selection Board had ever before been overruled, and he added:

"I thought we had such a clear cut and unanimous opinion all up and down the line that I was completely surprised at the decision."[10]

Admiral Anderson testified that McNamara's decision was a "surprise," and predicted that the Navy would end up with a plane too heavy to operate from the majority of aircraft carriers.[11] Admiral Anderson summed up his opinion of the TFX this way:

"The justification for the contract given [by McNamara] was intellectually dishonest."[12]

McNamara quickly retaliated against these two distinguished members of the Joint Chiefs of Staff for testifying before the Senate Committee. Admiral Anderson was dropped as head of the Navy, and General LeMay was reappointed for only one year instead of the customary two. This one year kept him silent during the 1964 political campaign.

Truth Or Career?

The best informed man on the technical merits of the competing General Dynamics and Boeing designs was Albert W. Blackburn of the Office of Defense Research and Engineering. He had been a Marine combat pilot, a North American Aviation test pilot, and held a Master's Degree in aeronautical engineering from M.I.T. He had been assigned to the TFX project for two years. After McNamara wrote his "Memorandum for the Record" overruling the Pentagon Source Selection Board, Blackburn wrote his own "Memorandum for the Record."[13] In doing this, he sacrificed his career for the cause of truth.

McNamara first tried to hide the Blackburn Memorandum from the McClellan Committee. Then McNamara stamped it "secret," hoping to keep it away from the Committee's investigators. Fortunately, the McClellan Committee already had a copy. As a final attempt to put the lid on Blackburn, he was ordered to concur in the General Dynamics decision. Blackburn personally protested this to Dr. Harold Brown, then director of Research and Engineering, and now Secretary of the Air Force. McNamara and Brown persisted in demanding that Blackburn concur in the General Dynamics decision, so Blackburn resigned, saying:

"I could no longer, in my conscience, remain associated with the Office of the Secretary of Defense."

Blackburn's "Memorandum for the Record," written March 1, 1963 while he was on duty in the Defense Department, stated emphatically:

"[The award to General Dynamics] could not in

any way be associated with the merits of the two
proposals on either an operational, technical, management, or cost basis. The *operational* commanders were the strongest in their support of the
Boeing design; however, the depth of *technical*
development of the Boeing design and its imagi-
native innovations such as thrust reversers, high-
lift devices (later adapted by General Dynamics)
and top-mounted engine inlets clearly pointed in
favor of their proposal. . . . From the *management*
point of view, the handling of such major Air
Force weapon systems as the B-47, B-52, and the
Minuteman, as well as the KC-135/707 development, must be considered superior to the management given the F-102, F-106, and the B-58
series and the notoriously poor management exercised in the General Dynamics jet transport
program. . . .

"Probably one of the most critical features of the
whole TFX exercise is the damage that may have
been wrought on our entire design competition
structure. It is difficult to imagine that several
hundred top technical experts from Wright Field
and the Bureau of Weapons would again with
such seriousness of purpose and over such a long
period of time, including many 7-day weeks, so
enthusiastically seek to accomplish the choice of
the superior weapon system proposal in another
such competition, when the total effort expended
by them is from their point of view completely
negated by an executive decision."

The Pentagon had asked for four separate
design submissions from the two companies.
Blackburn proved that, after *each* of the four
design submissions (January, May, June and September, 1962), Boeing was unanimously rated
both better and cheaper. He made clear that the
Pentagon request for the fourth submission was
to give General Dynamics additional time to try

to match the superior Boeing design. Blackburn wrote:

> "All the imaginative aerodynamic fixes devised by Boeing in their third submission to satisfy the very difficult Navy maneuver requirements somehow found their way into the final General Dynamics design to a degree of similarity that would hardly be coincidence."

In other words, the Pentagon gave General Dynamics every advantage, and someone even leaked "the superior design features submitted in a rival bid by the Boeing Company."[14] With this kind of inside assistance, General Dynamics finally produced a single aircraft design for the Air Force and Navy—but its weight was still about 2,000 pounds greater than the Boeing design.

Auditing McNamara's Head

After the Blackburn "Memorandum" had demolished all McNamara's technical arguments in favor of General Dynamics, McNamara tried a different type of lie. On April 20, 1963 he appeared before the American Society of Newspaper Editors and said that his TFX award

"will yield a saving of approximately $1 billion."

Senator McClellan asked the General Accounting Office to check this strange new cost figure just revealed by McNamara. The Comptroller General testified that his office could not find any cost records to substantiate McNamara's statement. The Director of Defense Accounting for the GAO, William A. Newman, quoted McNamara as saying "he had the figures in his head, indicating he did not have them on paper." Newman said he could not "audit figures in somebody's head."[15]

A knowledgeable reporter then asked McNamara how he could reject the Boeing bid and say it lacked "cost realism" when he admittedly had no cost studies on paper. McNamara arrogantly replied:

> "I'm a $500,000 a year executive. I was the second-highest paid accountant in the United States."[16]

McNamara was employed by the Ford Motor Company at the time President Kennedy appointed him Secretary of Defense. If McNamara made Ford's cost studies on the Edsel automobile "in his head" instead of on paper, it is no wonder that the Edsel proved to be such a fantastically costly mistake. And it is no wonder that Ford leaped at the chance to unload this "second-highest paid accountant" onto the Federal Government where deficits are welcomed.

Eating Their Words

The same bullet that killed President Kennedy in November 1963 also killed the Senate investigation of the TFX. By common consent, the Democrats agreed that they would not continue the investigation because it might reflect adversely on the memory of their dead President, who had fully backed McNamara's TFX decision.

As the years rolled on, optimistic progress reports poured forth from the Pentagon publicity staff. Just before the 1964 election, there was a gala "rollout" ceremony in Fort Worth to make the voters believe that everything was on schedule.

On May 11, 1965 at an impressive ceremony in New York, the first Navy TFX plane was rolled out. Secretary of the Navy Paul Nitze hailed the new plane as "a significant milestone." Test pilot Ralph Donnell predicted that TFX critics "are going to eat their words."[17]

The TFX was renamed the F-111. But Senators uncovered new evidence in 1967.

Senate investigators discovered that the stage-managed TFX production plane of May 11, 1965 was just as phony as all the other claims made for the General Dynamics plane. Senator McClellan said *that* plane was *not* the first Navy TFX at all, but "a wired-up thing for demonstration" hurriedly thrown together at a special cost of $1,417,029 in order to make a "great fanfare." The rear half was a Navy plane, and the front half was an Air Force plane. When questioned by McClellan, Paul Nitze suffered a sudden loss of memory. He just couldn't remember being present. But newspaper files contain photos of Nitze making a speech at the phony production plane "rollout."[18]

On December 10, 1965 at the LBJ Ranch in Texas, McNamara announced he planned to scrap 345 B-52 bombers and 80 B-58 bombers and replace them with 210 TFX bombers, which he called the FB-111. McNamara emphasized:

"The FB-111 will have twice the speed of those aircraft, approximately, with approximately the same range. . . . It will carry fifty 750-pound high-explosive bombs."

This was a triple lie. *When it is carrying bombs,* the FB-111 cannot fly any faster than the B-52. This is because the FB-111 is so small that its bombs must be hung from its wings. This creates enough "drag" to prevent the plane from flying any faster than the B-52.

Second, the FB-111 has *only half the range* of the B-52. The authoritative Air Force/Space Digest stated:

"Even the early B-52s . . . will fly more than 6,000 miles fully loaded. . . . With 48 bombs under its wings and carrying only internal fuel [the FB-111] couldn't exceed 2,500 miles. . . ."

McNamara's third lie is his statement that the

FB-111 will carry fifty 750-pound bombs. The FB-111 can carry six bombs from each of eight wing stations for a total of 48, provided its wings are fully extended. *When the "sweep wing" is swept back* for supersonic flight, the pilot must dump half his bomb load.

On April 4, 1966 the House Armed Services Committee issued a report which documented McNamara's lies about the FB-111. It concluded:

> "Regrettably, the statistics used by the Secretary of Defense to illustrate the claimed superiority of the FB-111 over the B-52 . . . and B-58 aircraft . . . had the net effect of *significantly misrepresenting* the comparative capability of these aircraft. . . ." (emphasis added)

General Curtis LeMay summed it up this way:

> "The FB-111 is by no stretch of the imagination a strategic bomber. . . . We are taking an awful risk [by relying on the FB-111]."[19]

In other words, even if the FB-111 eventually does fly, it will not be as good as the B-52s it will replace.

TFX = Total Fiasco 'Xpensive

The body of a drowning victim doesn't always rise to the surface immediately. Sometimes it takes a while. The year 1967 was a year when the dead bodies in the TFX scandal finally rose to the surface for public scrutiny.

Two TFX test planes were destroyed in crashes. The second crash, on April 21, 1967, killed test pilot Ralph Donnell who had believed what McNamara and his press agent, Arthur ("it's an inherent government right to lie") Sylvester had said about the TFX.

Navy Secretary Paul Nitze confessed, in answer to a question from Senator McClellan, that the TFX is two years behind schedule.[20]

The Pentagon conceded that the cost of the TFX program has doubled from $6.5 billion to $13 billion. Furthermore, the price tag now covers 400 fewer planes (1,300 instead of 1,700). Every failure of the General Dynamics plane to meet its specifications has resulted in loading the contract price with "extras" in a bureaucratic attempt to "explain" the increased costs.

The poor performance record of the TFX is just as startling as its cost and delay. Here is the picture as it unfolded in hearings before the Senate Defense Appropriation Subcommittee in the summer of 1967.[21]

1. The F-111 cannot dogfight with enemy aircraft.[22] When Air Force Lt. Gen. James Ferguson was asked by Senator McClellan what he would do if he encountered a Soviet MIG-21 while flying an F-111 over North Vietnam, Ferguson replied:

"I know what I would do. . . . I would go down on the deck and get out of there."

Other fighter planes will have to be built to do the job for which the TFX was originally intended.[23]

2. The F-111 can scarcely fly over Pikes Peak when fully loaded with the type bombs we are using in Vietnam.

3. The F-111 engine is subject to flameouts when the power-boosting afterburner is used.

4. The F-111 range is dramatically less than anticipated.[24]

The Navy version of the F-111 has all those problems, plus others. Senator McClellan reported to the Senate on August 22, 1967 that the Navy F-111 has 257 deficiencies and "remains unfit for service use" and "incapable of carrier-based operations." The Navy F-111 is nearly 10,000 pounds overweight, and 11,000 feet below its planned combat ceiling.

Hanson W. Baldwin, military editor of *The New York Times*, on August 11, 1967 set forth numerous technical troubles of the TFX. He said that, when testing the F-111 with half bomb loads, the vibrations were so severe that the pilot had difficulty in reading his instruments and "they were shaking the shackle pins off the bombs." Baldwin added, "One problem that has plagued the plane since it first flew—a sharp stalling or surging of the engine during flight—still persists."[25] The Pentagon acknowledged that Baldwin's article was accurate.[26]

The TFX failure is not completely the fault of General Dynamics' inferior design, higher cost factors, and management. Just as responsible is McNamara's personal directive that the TFX be one "common" plane to satisfy the different requirements of the Air Force and the Navy. Today, McNamara stubbornly insists that the TFX be an impossible mixture: a long-range bomber, a low-flying tactical bomber, a land-based fighter, and a carrier-based fighter. But as former Joint Chiefs Chairman Nathan F. Twining said:

"The resulting hybrid machine cannot perform any one of its missions in an optimum manner."[27]

More succinctly, the TFX is an all-purpose flop.

The record proves beyond a shadow of a doubt that there was no sound technical reason for McNamara's decision to grant the TFX contract to General Dynamics, and that Senator McClellan is right in calling it a "multi-billion dollar blunder." Why, then, was General Dynamics chosen? The answer is corrupt politics at its worst.

chapter VII

THE BIG PAYOFF

Nearly every generation in American politics has had its Boss Tweed of Tammany Hall (who died in jail), Boss Honey Fitzgerald of Boston (grandfather of the Kennedys who was refused his seat in Congress because of vote frauds), or Boss Pendergast of Kansas City (who went to the Federal penitentiary after putting his hand-picked candidate, Harry Truman, in the U.S. Senate).

The formula for building a political machine is

very simple: (1) award city contracts (for buildings, streets, printing, etc.) to favored contractors who tolerate payoffs and kickbacks, and (2) use the money this provides to pay off enough ward heelers to buy, steal or rig the election of all machine candidates. For example, Boss Tweed owned printing and marble businesses; Boss Pendergast owned the Ready-Mixed Concrete Company, which supplied all the highway and building projects ordered by County Commissioner Harry Truman.

The magnitude of the TFX corruption—both in political power and in financial payoffs—makes all the other graft in American history look like petty larceny.

Some people think that the Edsel automobile, on which the Ford Motor Company lost $250 million, was the biggest business loss in history. It wasn't. The largest financial loss in all corporate history was the $425 million General Dynamics lost on its Convair 880 and 990 jet transport planes. In 1962, just prior to the TFX award, General Dynamics was on the verge of bankruptcy. *Fortune Magazine*, in two articles in January and February, 1962, described its hopeless financial condition.

It is particularly significant that General Dynamics' bid was $415 million more than the Boeing bid—and that General Dynamics was then in the red for $425 million. Congressman Bill Stinson called these figures "amazingly similar." The amount by which the General Dynamics' bid exceeded the Boeing bid was approximately the amount General Dynamics needed to recoup its terrible loss.[1]

Winning the TFX contract, therefore, was a

matter of life-or-death survival for General Dynamics. Since GD obviously could not win on merit, it had to go another route to obtain this largest of all Government contracts. That other route was political. The most powerful political machines in the United States combined to take the TFX award away from Boeing and give it to General Dynamics.

The General Dynamics bid said that TFX would be built in Fort Worth, Texas, home state of Vice President Lyndon Johnson (24 electoral votes), with the Navy version built in New York (45 electoral votes). Additionally, what is not generally known, General Dynamics was controlled by the chairman of its Executive Committee and largest single stockholder, Henry Crown of Chicago, one of the most powerful financial figures in the Democrat machine in Illinois (27 electoral votes). The Boeing Company, on the other hand, is headquartered in Seattle, Washington (only 9 electoral votes), and, if Boeing had received the TFX contract, the plane would have been built in Wichita, Kansas (only 8 electoral votes).

In the very close presidential election of 1960, Washington and Kansas had gone for Richard Nixon—so obviously they were not eligible for Federal favors. Even looking ahead to the 1964 election, the Administration could afford to offend those states because their electoral votes were so few.

Texas, Illinois and New York, however, presented quite a different picture. In 1960, all three had voted for the Kennedy-Johnson ticket. Even more important, Texas and Illinois were the locations of shocking election frauds which put those states in the Kennedy-Johnson column by the narrowest of margins. (New York had gone Democrat in 1960 when Governor Nelson Rockefeller failed to give enthusiastic support to Richard Nixon.)

By the code of the political grafters, no states deserved the "spoils" more than Texas and Illinois. They had "delivered the vote" in a year when it wasn't easy to deliver. When speaking in Chicago in September 1964, Vice President Hubert Humphrey (who ought to know) paid the Cook County machine this very dubious compliment:

"You people in Chicago did more to elect Kennedy in 1960 than any other people in America."

Carrying Texas, Illinois and New York would be crucial to the reelection of the Kennedy-Johnson Administration in 1964. There was coolness between Kennedy and Johnson on some subjects. But on the matter of their own reelection in 1964, they were two politicians of a single mind. In a contract the size of the TFX, there was enough money to take care of everyone who needed to be taken care of. Nowhere in the United States could political money be used so effectively as through the Texas and Illinois machines. Their efficient, smooth-functioning, well-disciplined operation could get the job done and "keep the bodies buried."

Secretary McNamara knew that the reelection of the Kennedy-Johnson Administration was crucial to keeping his job as Secretary of Defense. Having enjoyed the second most powerful office in our country, he wasn't about to give it up. As explained by one of the most perceptive reporters in Washington:

"In the executive branch, McNamara had an equally keen sense for understanding the centers of power. His ardent attention was directed at President Kennedy, Attorney General Robert F. Kennedy, and Vice-President Johnson. From the outset, McNamara's Defense Department was well supplied with Johnson men."[2]

It was almost uncanny the way McNamara had courted Lyndon Johnson, and appointed his proteges to big jobs during the Kennedy years when everyone else was labelling Lyndon "the forgotten man" in Washington. Johnson men in the Pentagon included Secretary of the Army Cyrus Vance, Secretary of the Navy John B. Connally, Jr., and his successor, Secretary of the Navy Fred Korth.

The TFX award to General Dynamics was the political payoff to the machines which delivered the vote to the Kennedy-Johnson ticket in 1960. More than that, it was the guarantee that Texas, Illinois, and New York would deliver again in 1964.

"LBJ Saved The Day"

The news that the TFX contract would go to General Dynamics was known in Texas at a time when the Pentagon was telling Senators that the decision had not yet been made. On October 24, 1962—one month before the TFX award was announced—the *Fort Worth Press* ran a story saying it was informed by two "very high echelon people" in the Kennedy Administration that "General Dynamics of Fort Worth will get the multibillion-dollar defense contract to build the supersonic TFX." After this story appeared, Deputy Secretary of Defense Roswell Gilpatric solemnly assured Senators that no decision had yet been made.

It is not hard to speculate on who the "very high echelon people" were.

After the TFX contract was announced on November 24, 1962, the *Fort Worth Press* bragged about its scoop. It is significant that the newspaper did not claim foresight in its October 24 article. Nor did the paper claim it had made a lucky guess. The *Fort Worth Press* boasted that the reporter had been given "the official word" that "the deal had been wrapped up."

On December 12, 1962, Vice President Lyndon Johnson visited the General Dynamics plant in Fort Worth to take the credit for the TFX decision. As he made his grand entrance, he was greeted by signs which read:

LBJ SAVED THE DAY!
WE'RE HERE TO STAY, THANKS TO LBJ!
WE'VE GOT JOBS, THANKS TO THE
EFFORTS OF LBJ!

Waiting to greet LBJ in the lobby was the president of General Dynamics who had flown out from New York for the victory celebration.[3]

Political Power In Chicago

The public is generally unaware of the immense political power wielded by the Democrat machine in Chicago. This is not merely power to control elections and candidates. It is a far-reaching power which can do many things. The two anchormen in the Chicago Democrat organization are Democrat National Committeeman Jake Arvey and Henry Crown (the controlling owner of General Dynamics at the time of the TFX award). Crown owned Material Service Corp., which supplied most of the concrete for the public building and road jobs in Cook County.

Here is one example of what the Chicago machine can do. In 1963, Jake Arvey's son, 45-year-old Erwin B. Arvey, used $550,000 in forged General Motors Acceptance Corporation bonds as collateral to borrow fraudulently $400,000 from a Los Angeles bank, $160,000 from a St. Louis bank, and $60,000 from a Chicago bank. He pleaded guilty in the Federal courts in Los Angeles and St. Louis to the interstate transportation of counterfeit bonds, which "were falsely made, forged and counterfeited as defendant then and there well knew."[4]

Defendant Erwin B. Arvey never served a day in jail for any of these offenses. In lieu of the penitentiary penalty (up to ten years) the law provides for this offense, he was permitted by the Federal courts in Los Angeles and St. Louis to receive treatment at the Menninger Clinic in Topeka, Kansas, and then be released.[5] He was represented in St. Louis by his father and by attorney Morris Shenker, a prominent Democrat who was much in the news in 1967 as the liaison between Jimmy Hoffa and Senator Ed Long of Missouri. Shenker paid Long $48,000 while the Senator was investigating the alleged wiretapping of Hoffa by Treasury agents.[6]

The Chicago indictment of Arvey was voluntarily dismissed on December 21, 1963 by the Government because "it had no proof Arvey knew the bonds were stolen." This was *after* Arvey had pleaded guilty on December 9, 1963 in Los Angeles Federal court to knowing that the bonds were counterfeit.[7]

Richard Arvey, grandson of Jake Arvey, was able to reserve the use of the caucus room in the House of Representatives in the Capitol for David J. Miller, the convicted draft-card burner, to speak to several hundred Senate-House summer interns on July 13, 1967. When protests against this misuse of the caucus room were made, young Arvey said college students "have the right to hear." The Miller anti-draft talk was cancelled at the last minute by the horrified Speaker of the House, John W. McCormack.[8]

The corrupt influence of the Chicago Democrat machine is so powerful that it was able to kill many pages of President Johnson's 1967 Crime Commission Report. Professor G. Robert Blakey of the University of Notre Dame prepared a 63-page report on syndicated crime in the Chicago area for publication by this Commission. His report named *specific* links between Chicago Democrat officials and the organized crime syndicate. A Commission staff member said,

"There were protests from officeholders in Chicago and *enormous pressure* on us *not* to be specific."[9]

The Blakey Report, which was suppressed by the White House, concluded:

"The success of the Chicago group has been primarily attributable to its ability to corrupt the law enforcement processes, including police officials and members of the judiciary. . . . Control, sometimes direct, has been exercised over local, state and federal officials and representatives. Men have been told when to run or not run for office, or how to vote or not to vote on legislative issues, or [for judges] how to decide motions to suppress evidence or for judgments of acquittal."[10]

Now reread the formula given at the beginning of this chapter for building a political machine, and apply it to the TFX contract.

The Shuttle

The American public is constantly fed a line about how difficult it is to persuade qualified and successful men to take high Government positions because of low salaries. Few people realize how many use a Government job as a springboard to financial enrichment. One of the indicators of the decline in public morals is the contrast between

Herbert Hoover and Lyndon Johnson. Hoover's belief that "a public office is a public trust" was so high that he never accepted any salary the whole time he was President, and he even refused to permit his brilliant son to work for any company which had any business dealings with the Federal Government. On the other hand, Lyndon Johnson, during the years he was feeding at the public trough, amassed a fortune estimated at $14,000,000. As the slogan goes, "Does politics pay? Ask LBJ."

One of the lucrative ways that the "in" clique makes money while on the public payroll is the "profession" of shuttling back and forth between Government service and private business or law practice. A classic example was the way Under Secretary of State Dean Acheson in 1946 granted a $90 million U.S. loan to the Communist-controlled government of Poland over the strenuous protest of our U.S. Ambassador.[11] Acheson later admitted to a Senate Committee that he personally was responsible for approving the loan, that his own law firm represented the Red government of Poland in the negotiations, and that the Acheson law firm received a fee of more than $50,000 when the load was granted.[12]

A New York lawyer named Roswell Leavitt Gilpatric rode the "shuttle" between the Pentagon and the law firm of Cravath, Swaine & Moore. From 1958 to January 1961, Gilpatric, a partner in the firm, served as lawyer for General Dynamics. Officials of General Dynamics later testified that they had paid Gilpatric's law firm more than $300,000 from 1959 through March 1963.[13]

In January 1961, Gilpatric took a leave of absence from the firm to become Deputy Secretary of Defense, the No. 2 man in the Pentagon, second only to McNamara. Gilpatric claimed he had resigned from the firm, but Senate investigators proved that *while* he was Deputy Secretary of Defense, Gilpatric received $20,000 per year from the firm, and that the insurance for him and his secretary was continued pending his return.

Gilpatric was one of the four Pentagon civilians who overruled the Pentagon Source Selection Board and picked General Dynamics over Boeing to build the TFX. Gilpatric was the Pentagon official who actually signed the $6.5 billion TFX contract (which has since climbed to $13 billion). McNamara was out of the country, and the heat was on to sign the contract before the McClellan Committee began its investigation. Gilpatric signed it.

Immediately after the contract was signed, Gilpatric's law firm was named *the* general counsel for General Dynamics, and Gilpatric's partner, Maurice T. Moore, was named a director.

On January 9, 1964, Gilpatric resigned as Deputy Secretary of Defense and returned to his New York law firm, which was still representing General Dynamics for a fee of more than $100,000 a year.

Texas-Size Corruption

A Texas lawyer and banker named Fred Korth rode the "shuttle" between the Pentagon and the Continental Bank in Fort Worth, of which he was president. General Dynamics was one of the best customers of Korth's bank. In the fall of 1961, Korth arranged a $400,000 loan to General Dynamics—a very large loan, indeed, for a bank with a loan limit of $600,000.[14]

When Korth became Secretary of the Navy in

January 1962, he resigned as president of the Bank, but he kept $160,000 in bank stock. At the time of his appointment, Korth told the Senate Committee that he intended to return to the Bank at the end of his Government service.[15]

Korth then became one of the little clique that awarded the TFX to General Dynamics, thus overruling the recommendation of every Pentagon evaluation team. Korth later testified that he had not read the evaluation reports on TFX before he overruled them. Senate investigators discovered, on the other hand, that Korth, after becoming Navy Secretary, had 21 conferences and telephone contacts with General Dynamics officials.

As Secretary of the Navy, Korth continued his enthusiastic assistance to the Continental Bank. Senate investigators produced letters promoting business for the Bank which Korth had written on official Navy stationery. The investigation also turned up correspondence from the Continental Bank thanking Korth for bringing in $20,000 and $30,000 accounts.

Korth's activities violated the code against "conflict of interest." Senator Simpson of Wyoming summed up the reaction of all who heard the testimony:

> "Why did General Dynamics need the loan? It had undergone the largest corporate loss of any business concern in American history. Why does General Dynamics now seem to have a glowing future? It is because Mr. Korth participated in the decision that gave General Dynamics . . . the largest contract in our history. . . . Can there be any question that Mr. Korth's conduct was improper, injudicious and suspect?"[16]

President Kennedy defended Korth to the end, but Korth had to go. His conduct was too raw for any other Democrats to defend. To cover his hasty exit from Washington, a trumped-up story was circulated about an alleged dispute with McNamara over nuclear carriers. Nobody fell for it.

After General Dynamics received the TFX award, the $400,000 loan was repaid to the Continental Bank of Fort Worth.

The Higher Bid Usually Wins

On August 9, 1967, Congressman Otis G. Pike of New York held a press conference and exhibited five items which the Defense Department had bought at prices ranging from 400% to 5,000% above the manufacturer's list price. He showed nuts and bolts available in any hardware store for 6¢ for which the Pentagon paid $1.55.

Secretary McNamara promptly issued a sarcastic blast designed to belittle Pike for daring to question Pentagon purchases.

But Pike wasn't cowed. He came back with the hard evidence that the Defense Department had bought 130 generator knobs for $33,398.95, when the manufacturer's catalogue listed the price at $212.60.

By August 31, an embarrassed McNamara was beating a hasty retreat. He conceded that Pike had uncovered a scandal whereby Designatronics, Inc. of Mineola, New York had overcharged the Defense Department by $50,000 to $75,000 on $750,000 worth of equipment over the last three years.[17]

Pike had driven the opening wedge. Many Congressmen then said they have received complaints of cases indicating fraud as well as inefficiency. Most complaints involved small businesses which were frozen out of defense contracts by big corporations with influence in Washington.

...ays seems to turn out that the ... influential company receiving the ...s higher than the bid of the company ...t get it. For example, a Philadelphia ...ny lost out on a $10 million contract for ...able radios although its bid was $884,856 ...er than the successful bidder, the giant Radio Corporation of America.[18] There are more than 100 similar cases awaiting the attention of Congressional investigations.[19]

In September 1967 when Congressman John Byrnes successfully knocked out of the budget an appropriation to buy some high-priced British ships, he created an international incident that brought to light another skeleton in the TFX closet.

In order to lower the apparent cost per plane, and to deceive Congress into believing that the TFX is wanted by the Royal Air Force, McNamara twisted the arm of the British government to order a number of General Dynamics planes. As explained by economist Eliot Janeway from Switzerland, where the deal was well known:

> "He [McNamara] guaranteed delivery of a brand new air fleet for less than nothing. . . . His formula . . . was to pay England more for other defense business than we charged her for the TFX. One of the small 'offset' orders guaranteed to England as part of the TFX package was for small ships."[20]

Although ⅔ of the cost of the TFX planes had already been covered by U.S. purchases from Britain, Britain threatened to renege on the deal when faced with the possibility of paying anything for the TFX planes.[21]

chapter VIII

THE INJUSTICE DEPARTMENT

When the newly-elected President John Kennedy in December 1960 announced the appointment of his brother, Bobby, as U.S. Attorney General, widespread criticism generally focused on three points: his lack of experience, his youth, and the fact that he was the President's brother. Now with the benefit of hindsight, we can see that there was another reason why this appointment was bad—Bobby, having been the presidential campaign manager, brought politics into the Justice Department.

Americans have long tolerated the custom that the President's campaign manager could be rewarded with a Cabinet post. The job usually deemed appropriate was that of Postmaster General (e.g., James Farley and Robert Hannegan), where he could dispense patronage to the victors. The extent of harm a politician could do in this position was limited to loading the Post Office payroll. The mails were still carried fairly for the "outs" as well as the "ins."

The appointment of Robert Kennedy, the politician, to head the Justice Department began a new period in American politics. Patronage was a minor attribute of his new Government job. This began the era when politics controlled enforcement of the law. The new Attorney General was a politician who used the Justice Department as a political arm of the Administration.

In recent years, concerned Americans have become indignant about the decisions of the Warren Supreme Court which have opened the jails and released hundreds of criminals and Communists. Equally serious is the failure of the Justice Department to enforce the laws we do have. In the heyday of radio, one of the popular programs was *Mr. District Attorney*. Each week's show opened by reminding listeners that the duty of the D.A. was to prosecute to the fullest extent of the law all persons accused of crime. Under Robert Kennedy and his successors, this is exactly what the Justice Department has failed to do.

Conflict Of Interest

In the Dixon-Yates case, the Supreme Court

ruled that the purpose of the "conflict of interest" law is to prevent Federal employees "from advancing their own interests at the expense of the public welfare."[1] The U.S. law against "conflict of interest" states:

> "*Acts Affecting A Personal Financial Interest.* . . . Whoever, being an officer or employee of the executive branch of the United States Government, . . . participates personally and substantially as a Government officer or employee, through decision, approval, disapproval, recommendation, the rendering of advice, investigation, or otherwise, in a judicial or other proceeding, application, request for a ruling or other determination, contract, claim, controversy, charge, accusation, arrest, or other particular matter in which, to his knowledge, he, his spouse, minor child, partner, organization in which he is serving as officer, director, trustee, partner or employee, or any person or organization with whom he is negotiating or had any arrangement concerning prospective employment, *has a financial interest* —
> "Shall be fined not more than $10,000 or imprisoned not more than two years, or both."[2]

In the presidential campaign of 1960, the Democrats made political hay out of the "conflict of interest" in the Dixon-Yates case. But the Dixon-Yates case was just "small change" compared to the big money and the gross violations involved in the TFX case.

The "conscience of the Senate," Senator John J. Williams, called to the attention of the Attorney General the action of Roswell Gilpatric in awarding the TFX contract to General Dynamics while he was being paid secret fees by the law firm which represented General Dynamics, and in which he was a partner both before and after he awarded the TFX contract. Senator Williams asked if these facts constituted a violation of the criminal law on conflict of interest and of President Kennedy's conflict-of-interest order of July 15, 1962.

The "conscience of the House," Congressman H. R. Gross, said that Fred Korth was guilty of a "clear conflict of interest" and "this is a real Texas-size raid on the U.S. defense budget."[3]

Although the laws prohibiting conflicts of interests by Federal employees, which the Eisenhower Administration successfully invoked in the Dixon-Yates case, are on the books and have been strengthened, no prosecution of the Pentagon civilians who profited from the TFX contract was ever started or even considered by the Kennedy-Johnson Administration.

Insurrection

When General Edwin Walker, a West Point graduate who fought for his country in the Aleutians, on Anzio Beach, in France, and in Korea, went to Oxford, Mississippi on September 30, 1962 to observe what was happening, Attorney General Robert Kennedy and Deputy Attorney General Nicholas Katzenbach moved with lightning speed to arrest him on the false charges of insurrection, opposing Federal officials, and seditious conspiracy. On the long-distance "diagnosis" of a Government psychiatrist (who had never seen Walker, but only read about him in the newspaper), the Kennedy-Katzenbach team denied bail to Walker and whisked him in the dead of night across state lines to the Federal prison for the insane at Springfield, Missouri. There he was put in solitary confinement and his bail fixed at $100,000.

So ridiculous and false was the case against

General Walker that Kennedy and Katzenbach dismissed all charges against him on January 21, 1963.[4] A court-appointed psychiatrist found Walker sane and possessed of "a superior level of intelligence."

Now compare this action against the much-decorated General Walker with the refusal of the Justice Department to take any action against the flagrant insurrection and sedition that took place in the long, hot summer of 1967.

When Stanley Wise, executive secretary of SNCC, made a speech at the Center for the Study of Democratic Institutions in Santa Barbara, California in August 1967 stating that his organization was "absolutely without doubt responsible for the race riots throughout the country," that "the institutions of this country must be destroyed," and proclaimed himself dedicated to getting Negro soldiers in U.S. bases around the world to quit their jobs—no one was prosecuted.[5]

Rap Brown, national chairman of SNCC, screamed in a speech in Washington, D.C. on July 27, 1967:

> "Get you some guns. If necessary, burn this town down. . . . The white man is your enemy. You got to destroy your enemy. . . . I say there should be more shooting than looting so if you loot, loot a gun store."

Yet, the Justice Department did not prosecute.

When Stokely Carmichael advised young men to "say 'hell no' to the draft,"[6] and made all the other violent speeches quoted in Chapter III—no one was prosecuted. Former Supreme Court Justice Charles E. Whittaker gave as his opinion:

> "I have no doubt whatever that Mr. Carmichael has thereby violated existing federal statutes, and, of course, such violations constitute a basis for

his prosecution under those statutes so violated."[7]

The Communist *Worker* exulted:

"The rebellion of the slums of Detroit, like all previous upsurges, was marked by the 'liberation' of foodstuff and needed household appliances and furniture. The picture windows of the stores . . . taunt and challenge the prisoners of the slums to an act of re-distribution, of some token 'sharing of the wealth.'

"In truth, the uprising in the slums of the big cities during this month — historically revolutionary July! — renders a dramatic service to the country."[8]

Yet, no one was prosecuted for inciting looting, rioting and insurrection.

Not a single person has been arrested or prosecuted by the Justice Department under the laws against insurrection, sedition and seditious conspiracy which were invoked against General Walker. (The State of Maryland is trying to put Brown behind bars, but that does not relieve the Justice Department of its duty.)

The Warren Court freed convicted Communists on the ground that advocating the overthrow of the Government by force and violence was not punishable so long as it was "divorced from any effort to instigate action to that end."[9] Even under this most tortured ruling of the Warren Court, Carmichael and Brown should be prosecuted. They are not only advocating overthrow of the Government by force and violence, but their "effort to instigate action to that end" is immediate and obvious. Riots have erupted within hours, and sometimes within minutes, after their speeches. The Justice Department has only to take their words at face value.

But Attorney General Ramsey Clark and the

Justice Department are afflicted with a strange
case of legal paralysis. They simply refuse to enforce any of the laws prohibiting insurrection and
seditious conspiracy against any of the inciters of
the riots.

Political Contributions

Senator John J. Williams has repeatedly stated
that the Justice Department has refused to enforce
the existing law against political donations by
unions. He pointed out that the *St. Louis Globe-
Democrat* has documented political gifts by the
Steamfitters union, in violation of the law, of at
least $80,000 to Democrat candidates in nine states
in 1964, including $52,000 to President Johnson's
1964 campaign fund and $10,000 to Robert
Kennedy.[10] Senator Williams said:

> "Just how they [Justice Department] officials could
> rule that they [Steamfitter officials] would not
> have to report, I am at a loss to understand."[11]

Instead of prosecution, Attorney General Robert
Kennedy arranged for President Johnson to com-
mute the sentence of the previously-convicted
Steamfitter boss, Lawrence L. Callanan.[12]

In September 1967, Secretary of Transportation
Alan S. Boyd called a meeting of executives of cor-
porate shippers, truckers, and airlines, at a private
club in Washington. He urged them to support
President Johnson for another term. Then the executives were asked to buy $1,000-a-couple tickets
to a Democrat fund-raising dinner to be held in
Washington on October 7. Thus, Government-
regulated corporations would most probably be the
ultimate source of political contributions of not
less than $1,000 each, made with the approval of
the President's new Cabinet officer.

This is clearly a violation of the spirit, if not
the letter, of the Corrupt Practices Act which for-

bids political contributions by corporations. It is also nothing but a "high-level lug" put on corporations which must stay in the good graces of the Administration in order to stay in business.[13]

But everyone knows that friends of the LBJ Administration are not subject to the same laws as everyone else. On the evening of October 7, 1964 Walter Jenkins, the No. 1 presidential assistant, was arrested at the Washington YMCA on a morals charge. This was his second offense on the same charge at the same place. The Department of Justice did not prosecute and he was allowed to forfeit his bond of $50 rather than go to trial.

Pornography For Profit

President Johnson told the Police Chiefs in Kansas City on September 14, 1967:

"I just don't believe that morality is declining."

This denial of all the evidence was more than Billy Graham could stand. Speaking in Kansas City that same night, Reverend Graham, who is better qualified to judge morality than LBJ, told his Crusade that morality in America *is* declining. He gave as proof the huge increase in crime and in pornography for sale on our public newsstands.

The Wall Street Journal reported that mail order smut business in 1967 is "unusually profitable" and is "large and growing." It said that the Post Office received 197,277 complaints of obscene mailings last year, triple the number in 1962.[14]

All this filth could be stopped by the Department of Justice. Federal laws forbid the mailing of any obscene, lewd or indecent publication.[15] Even the Warren Supreme Court recently ruled that, in enforcing these laws, the courts could consider the "commercial exploitation of erotica" and whether there is "a business of pandering to the

widespread weakness for titillation by pornography."[16]

The widespread failure to enforce the Federal
obscenity statutes raises a suspicion of payoffs from
the profits of this lucrative business.

Communist Subversion

During the 1940s and 1950s, the various
Attorney Generals published official lists of Com-
munist-front organizations for the guidance of
security officers and the public. On the last-
published list, 312 Communist fronts were named.
Attorney General Robert Kennedy did not add a
single name to the list, and neither did his successors Nicholas Katzenbach or Ramsey Clark.
Not one of the vicious Communist fronts openly
operating inside our country since 1960, such as
the Fair Play for Cuba Committee (one of whose
members assassinated President Kennedy), has
been added by any of the Democrat Attorney
Generals.

Congress has enacted many laws to insure
domestic tranquillity and to provide for the common defense. The Smith Act of 1940, the Internal
Security Act of 1950, the Communist Control Act
of 1954, and other sections of the U.S. Criminal
Code, were designed to protect us from subversives. The American people deserve enforcement
of these laws by the people hired and paid for
that purpose in the Justice Department. As the
U.S. Supreme Court said (before it was Warren-
ized) in upholding the convictions of Eugene
Dennis, Gus Hall and the other top Communists
in 1951:

"If Government is aware that a group aiming at
its overthrow is attempting to indoctrinate its
members and to commit them to a course
whereby they will strike when the leaders feel

the circumstances permit, *action by the Government is required*. . . . Certainly an attempt to overthrow the Government by force, even though doomed from the outset because of inadequate numbers or power of the revolutionists, is a sufficient evil for Congress to prevent."[17] (emphasis added)

The Department of Justice is subversion blind. The motto seems to be: See no Communists, hear no Communists. In November 1964, the Russian Embassy in Washington issued a pamphlet signed by Boris H. Ponomorev, head of the Foreign Section, Central Committee of the USSR, which said: "The Revolution in the United States has begun."

The Communist *Worker* carried a picture on November 6, 1966 of top U.S. Communists Gus Hall and Arnold Johnson meeting in the Kremlin with Soviet bosses Leonid Brezhnev, Mikhail Suslov, and Boris Ponomorev to plan what Ponomorev calls "Revolution in the USA."

Still the Justice Department will not prosecute.

Lt. General Arthur G. Trudeau, former Chief of Army Intelligence, testified on May 24, 1967:
"I can state that nearly all of the radical student organizations, the so-called pacifist organizations, and civil rights groups are honeycombed with Communists. . . .
"The riots and demonstrations in this country *are part of the Communist pressure techniques*. More battles will be timed to coincide with these demonstrations. *Mr. Suslov and Mr. Ponomorev will order bloodshed even in the United States as it suits their timing*. Therefore, I wish to make an unequivocal statement that the demonstrations in the streets of the cities of the United States are a force in direct support of the Viet Cong killing our troops in Vietnam; *and the leaders are taking orders and being supplied from the identi-*

*cal high command — the Central Committee of
the Communist Party of the USSR.*"[18] (emphasis
added)

But still the Justice Department does not enforce
our laws against any of the Communists in our
country. It has even dropped all of the charges
brought against Communists, Communist front organizations, and the Communist Party itself,
during the Eisenhower Administration.

Some may argue that it is no use for the Justice
Department to prosecute Communists because the
Warren Court will throw out any convictions. As
stated by the Chairman of the Senate Judiciary
Committee on May 2, 1962, and not refuted by any
Senator, the Warren Court has *sustained* the position advocated by the Communists in 46 important
cases. Since then, the Warren Court has ruled in
favor of the Communists in additional cases.

Nevertheless, we still have important laws
against subversion and Communist activity which
can be enforced by the Justice Department. Convictions could be obtained if the Attorney General
would put forth 1/10 of the energy, the per-
sistence, and the legal resourcefulness that he
exerts against anti-Communists such as the Cuban
freedom fighters. For example, an unprecedented
amount of Justice Department funds and time
were expended to secure the conviction of Richard
A. Lauchli, Jr. for selling guns in alleged violation
of the Federal Firearms Act. Lauchli thought he
was selling the reconditioned guns to Cuban freedom fighters to be used only against Castro and
outside the U.S. The buyers turned out to be
Federal agents who had entrapped him. The Government used similar strategy to indict and convict
leaders of the misguided little anti-Communist
group called the Minutemen. If such legal re-

sourcefulness were directed against the Communists, the Justice Department could secure convictions despite the Warren Court.

There would be enormous benefits to our country if the Justice Department made the proper attempt to enforce the laws against Communists:

1. It would break the financial back of the U.S. Communist Party by imposing enormous burdens of money and time on the Reds to defend themselves.

2. It might change the whole tenor of the Supreme Court, because it is unlikely that the Justices would care to face public reaction against the actual release of *thousands* of convicted Communists, instead of only dozens scattered out over the past ten years.

3. The mere investigation, indictment, and prosecution of Communists is of great public benefit because of its educational value. The lengthy and well-publicized trials of Alger Hiss, Gerhart Eisler, William Remington, the Rosenbergs, and the first and second string Communists, together with the testimony of undercover FBI agents, gave Americans a good look at the powerful and clever forces working to destroy us. We need this educational work brought up to date.

America is waiting for an Attorney General who will enforce the law—and a President with the courage to demand that he do so. The preservation of law and order is one of *the* decisive issues of our time. We will never have law and order unless we make this a political issue and elect *only* national, state and local candidates who are *pledged* to prosecute the guilty regardless of their political and propaganda power.

chapter IX

LEADERSHIP: CORRUPT OR MORAL?

ALL THESE THINGS WILL I GIVE THEE!

POWER

MONEY

PRAISE FROM LIBERAL PRESS

Why don't our government officials speak out against the corruption and the dangers that imperil our country today? This is the question that perplexes everyone when he awakens to what has happened to America.

At most other times in our history, there have been courageous leaders who spoke out on vital issues. There has always been some kind of a power-hungry clique. But there have also been leaders who dared to challenge the establishment. When Woodrow Wilson in 1918, with all the power of his Administration, tried to put over the League of Nations, many fell in step behind him; but there were also courageous men of both parties who spoke out against him. The great Senator James Reed of Missouri took on the task of "defying the lightning" and, with a tiny band of fearless fighters, did battle with the whole liberal internationalist establishment. Senator Reed is proof that we once had men of real courage in the Senate who were willing to stake their careers in a cause they believed was just.[1]

When Franklin Roosevelt proposed his "court-packing" bill in 1937, men of both parties opposed him with outraged indignation and defeated this grab for power.

Yet, today, when Administration officials are guilty of corruption, power-grabbing, and betrayal (such as trading with the enemy which is shipping supplies to kill American boys in Vietnam), there is a great deafening silence from those who should speak out.

Once a machine is funded by the formula described in Chapter VII, here is how it consolidates its control and silences its critics. The tactics are largely the same on the national level and in the big-city machines.

1. Use the power of the machine to elect and appoint handpicked candidates who are beholden to the machine.

2. Systematically promote to high office men with weaknesses for money, sex, alcohol, or power, so they can be intimidated and blackmailed.

3. Freeze out from positions of leadership anyone who is *not* beholden to the machine.

4. Try to compromise everyone in some way, even a small way.

5. Keep men "in line" with a combination of the carrot (the prospect of some political or financial favor) and the stick (the threat of having the smearbund expose and vilify their private lives).

The ability of a machine to put this bribe-and-blackmail strategy into effect, and to use it successfully and efficiently, is in direct proportion to the amount of public funds at its disposal. It is the tremendous Federal spending power which is the immediate cause of the rampant corruption in Washington today. To paraphrase Lord Acton's famous dictum: The spending power corrupts, and absolute spending power corrupts absolutely.

The American voters don't hear about the bribes and the blackmail—because who is going to tell on himself? Such offers are not usually made to the handful who are known to be incorruptible. Even those who resist entrapment are silenced by the examples of what happened to Senators Joseph McCarthy and Thomas Dodd. Only very, very occasionally does anyone on the inside lift the curtain and tell the public how the system works. Such a man was Martin Dies.

Up On The Mountain

In 1938 Martin Dies was one of the most promising young men in politics. He was a Democrat Congressman from Texas, the home of many powerful politicians. He was one of the top speakers in the country—one of a handful of Congressmen for whom the galleries were always filled when it was known that he would speak. He belonged to the Party in power when the Roosevelt Administration was riding high. If Dies had followed the path of personal ambition, he could easily have been where his fellow Texan, Lyndon Johnson, is today.

But Dies was a patriot who believed in defending America against our internal enemies. In 1938 he asked Congress to set up the House Committee on Un-American Activities, and he became its first chairman. With his Committee, he conscientiously set about the task of exposing Communists and what they were trying to do to our country.

The Reds immediately made Dies the target of a vicious campaign of harassment. He received many threats that his son would be kidnapped; one kidnapping attempt was made, which fortunately was not successful. His wife received a steady stream of anonymous telephone calls at night. The caller would make remarks such as "Well, is your husband dead yet?" and "I'm doing a lot of praying, but not for what you think. I am praying that Dies dies." Dies' enemies laid a clever trap to catch him with a beautiful woman, they used forged documents to smear him as a Fascist, and they planted Nazi agents on him. All these ploys were unsuccessful. One of the principal witnesses who was to appear before the Dies Committee, General Walter Krivitsky, was murdered in a Washington, D.C. hotel room by the Communist secret police.

Then one day in 1940 Dies received a telephone call from President Franklin Roosevelt asking him to come to the White House. When Dies arrived for this little tete-a-tete, Roosevelt used all his famous charm to cajole Dies into stopping his investigation of Communism. Roosevelt talked to Dies like a son, called him "Martin", and pictured for him the great rewards that the Administration could give if Dies would only "go along" and abandon the Committee on Un-American Activities. Roosevelt continued:

"You know, Martin, I have been watching you for a long time. You have a promising future. You are an able speaker and a young man and I want vigorous, able young men in the New Deal, and you can go a long way working with me. You have got to be loyal to me. I can't work with men that I can't depend upon. You can't go through with this investigation. . . . If you expose the Communists in the CIO, the CIO will turn against the Democratic Party. If we lose the CIO support in the eastern states, we cannot win."[2]

If ever there was a case of Lucifer taking a man up on the mountain and saying, "All these things will I give thee," this was it.

When Dies later described the meeting, he said: "I was somewhat weakened, to tell the truth. It sounded awfully good to me, what he was telling me, and being human, I am not going to represent myself as any hero, because I wasn't. I was just plain scared."

Dies was too modest. He was a hero. He turned down Roosevelt's tempting offer. Roosevelt then became angry and started calling him "Mr. Congressman." Finally Dies left, went right to a Committee hearing, and continued his investigation with all his energies.

In 1941, Dies ran for the Senate. And who do you think was the Roosevelt Administration's hand-picked candidate to defeat him? None other than Congressman Lyndon Baines Johnson, one of the Administration's errand boys. Roosevelt assigned Benjamin Cohen to tell Federal departments to get behind Lyndon's campaign and to pass the word to their underlings. FDR assigned

Thomas Corcoran to solicit campaign funds for LBJ from all businesses with Government contracts. With ample funds, LBJ hired a burlesque show to travel with him and raffled off a free Government bond at each political meeting. Presumably this compensated for Johnson's poor speeches. Dies might have won in spite of the Roosevelt Administration, but he was betrayed by the Governor of Texas, who entered the race at the last minute, and was elected.

Dies still had his seat in Congress, but by 1943 the Roosevelt Administration decided to purge him from political life. The Administration awarded large Government contracts to industries in Dies' district, and then brought in workers from other states. This resulted in 10,000 new voters, all beholden to the Administration, enough to swing the Congressional district. Influential people in the district were told that, if they would get rid of Dies, the district would receive more Federal spending. WPA pointedly cancelled a $350,000 grant for a causeway at Port Arthur that had already been authorized.[3]

Seven years of pressure and abuse finally exacted their toll. When in 1944 Dies developed a sore on his larynx which he thought was malignant, disgusted and exhausted, he announced his retirement. (More than 10 years later, his health partially restored, Dies was again re-elected to Congress from Texas. But it is significant that the Democrats never permitted him to return to the House Committee on Un-American Activities which he founded.)

Inflation In Corruption

Since that day in 1940 when Roosevelt took Dies up on the mountain, the power base of the incumbent Administration to make tempting bribes —and to impose sanctions on those who do not knuckle under—is now 15 times as great. This represents the increase in the spending power of the Federal Government from 1940 to 1967.

Furthermore, in the White House in 1967 was a man whose unscrupulous use of political power to achieve his objectives is so total that he makes Franklin Roosevelt look like an amateur.

Nobody talks about it, but only the utterly naive could believe that this same sort of carrot-and-stick manipulation of Congressmen is not multiplied a hundredfold. The long fingers of the liberal machine reach out through politics, business, finance and propaganda to force men to act and vote under orders. This hidden control causes the sickness that is popularly referred to as "Potomac fever"—the change that comes over those who live in Washington when they start doing whatever is expedient in order to remain there.

Many a vote in Congress has been changed by the adroit dangling of a Federal job or judgeship. If the Senator or Congressman "plays ball" with the Administration and votes right, the White House lets the Senator name his partner or friend or contributor to a vacancy. If the constituents fail to reelect the Congressman who succumbs to pressure, the Administration takes care of him with a Federal appointment.

Secretary of Defense McNamara has the fantastic authority to spend more than *$1 billion per week*. This is power such as no other man in history has ever had. It is power to make or break any Congressman—by opening or closing a military base, or by granting or denying a defense contract, or by a thousand indirect ways. This is power to silence all criticism on the great medium of television. No TV programs can warn the American people of what McNamara is doing to our defense because the corporations which can afford to sponsor such advertising cannot risk having their profits turned into losses by McNamara's spending power.

McNamara silences his critics in the military—the ones most qualified to expose his tactics—by a ruthless implementation of the *Fulbright Memorandum* which ordered the "muzzling of the military." For example, in January 1967, the Commandant of the Air War College, Major General Jerry D. Page, in a closed seminar for senior officers, made some mild statements about bomb shortages in Vietnam. For this alleged "criticism" of McNamara's policies, General Page was immediately banished from this prestige post to Okinawa (known as the U.S. equivalent of Siberia).[4] McNamara's message is quite clear—those who want choice assignments can keep their mouths shut.

As an example of how the going price in bribes has inflated with the times, we have the stunning revelation made on August 10, 1967 by President Hastings Kamuzu Banda of the African state of Malawi. He told a press conference that Red China had tried to bribe him to grant diplomatic recognition. Banda told how Red China's ambassador to Tanzania, Ho Ying, had approached him several times and offered him "a 6-million-pound bribe, which was later raised to 18 million pounds."[5]

This bribe of approximately $50 million is a fantastic fortune to be offered for the privilege of opening an embassy in the little country of Malawi, which has a population about the size of Chicago.

It took great strength of character to resist such a bribe.

Two questions naturally arise. How many others have accepted similar bribes from the Reds? And, if diplomatic recognition by the little state of Malawi was worth $50 million to the Reds, how much would the Reds pay for U.S. diplomatic recognition? The Red China lobby in the U.S. has been promoting the recognition of Red China ever since 1947, and has failed only because American public opinion is so overwhelmingly opposed.

In The Highest Places

How can we have high moral standards in Washington when the President of the United States had as his two closest friends and business associates throughout his adult life—Bobby Baker (convicted of income tax evasion, theft, and conspiracy to defraud the Government), and Walter Jenkins (a morals offender)?

The press, which for years had been shielding the sanctimonious public image of LBJ, suddenly couldn't take it any more and began to peel off the wrapper. Well-known members of the liberal Washington press corps revealed him as a man who is coarse, crude and cunning, vain, vulgar and vicious; they described his vile language, his scatological jokes, his terrible temper tantrums, his holding some business conferences in the bathroom, and the humiliating way he treats his employees. Johnson's obsession with his own grandeur is such that he bugs the phone lines of his employees, and he "deliberately spat liquor over a top aide who served him bourbon instead of his favorite Cutty Sark scotch."[6]

Justices of the Supreme Court have brought the

Court to a new level, not only by their criminal-and-Communist-coddling decisions, but by their own personal conduct. Chief Justice Earl Warren indulges in such petty chiseling as to call his wife a social worker in order to get the Government to finance a free trip to South America.[7] In October 1966, Senator Williams revealed that Justice William O. Douglas was being paid $12,000 a year by the Albert B. Parvin group, which owns an interest in four Las Vegas gambling casinos. Williams asked whether Douglas should "be permitted to remain on the Supreme Court."[8] Others said that the much-married Justice needed this addition to his $39,500 salary in order to support his four wives.

The Bobby Baker case lifted the curtain briefly on the tangled web of payoffs and pressures in which so many in Washington are caught. Insurance agent Don B. Reynolds testified on the morning of November 23, 1963 that Walter Jenkins required him to buy $1,208 worth of useless radio advertising time on the LBJ Company station in Austin, Texas, and give a $900 Magnavox stereo player to the Johnson family. He testified that Lady Bird Johnson selected the stereo from a catalogue sent to her by Bobby Baker. Then the establishment went into high gear to punish Reynolds for telling the truth. Secretary of Defense Robert McNamara and Attorney General Bobby Kennedy permitted confidential U.S. Air Force and FBI files on Don Reynolds to be leaked to Drew Pearson and *The New York Times* for the purpose of destroying Reynolds' credibility.[9]

Another scandal which is crying for exposure is the extent of homosexual infiltration of our Government. Perverts are easy targets for blackmail, and therefore are security risks. The lid was first publicly lifted when Senator Joseph McCarthy forced the State Department to concede that it had employed 145 homosexuals.

Since then, the fact that perversion has increased to epidemic proportions is confirmed by no less an authority than Justices William O. Douglas and Abe Fortas who said in a Supreme Court dissenting opinion on May 22, 1967:

"It is common knowledge that in this century homosexuals have risen high in our own public service — both in Congress and in the Executive Branch. . . ."[10]

Drawing The Line

There are a few fearless investigators in Congress today. One is Senator John McClellan, Democrat from Arkansas. McClellan is almost solely responsible for the investigation of the TFX, an investigation in which he persisted in spite of every temptation and every obstacle. If it hadn't been for McClellan, we would know very little of the TFX scandal recounted in Chapter 6. In spite of all the pressures from those who benefited financially from the TFX contract, as well as from the Administration eager for a coverup, McClellan never abandoned his search for the truth. It is too bad we can't say the same for some others on his Committee. The majority did a disappearing act when the time came to issue a report.

Another courageous Senator is Karl Mundt, Republican from South Dakota. He has done more than anyone to expose and document the blood traffic by which U.S. businesses sell to Communist countries strategic items which find their way into the bodies of American boys.

Another incorruptible Congressman is H. R. Gross, Republican from Iowa. Instead of joining in the gay Washington social life, he spends his evenings reading the fine print in the bills presented to Congress. He discovers many loopholes and payoffs, and then exposes them. Federal bureaucrats are panicky when he speaks; they can't retaliate because they can't get anything on him.

There are others. It is remarkable that we have as many as we do who don't succumb to Potomac fever.

The urgent need today is to develop and support leaders on every level of government who are independent of the bossism of every political machine—the big-city machine, the liberal Democrat machine, and the Republican kingmaker machine. This can be done by supporting *only* candidates who have moral integrity and the moral courage to keep their independence.

We are *not* going to support any candidate who lacks the moral courage to clean up the mess in Washington. We have had enough of those who betrayed our national defenses for political payoffs, who are afraid to speak out against big-city crime and riots, who are getting some secret subsidy on the side, or who have a moral skeleton in the closet. We are not going to accept for nomination men who have to hide behind the slogan "My personal life is none of your business," or whose record shows that they lack the moral integrity and political courage to oppose the twin evils of crime and Communism.

chapter X

WHY DON'T WE WIN IN VIETNAM?

STRATEGIC TARGETS IN NORTH VIET NAM

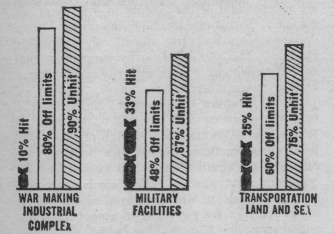

WAR MAKING INDUSTRIAL COMPLEX — 10% Hit, 80% Off limits, 90% Unhit

MILITARY FACILITIES — 33% Hit, 48% Off limits, 67% Unhit

TRANSPORTATION LAND AND SEA — 25% Hit, 60% Off limits, 75% Unhit

The United States has been engaged in a shooting war in Vietnam *almost* as long as we were engaged in a shooting war in World War II, when we completely defeated two very powerful enemies on two distant fronts. After 3⅓ years of World War II, we had Germany and Japan on their knees; after 3⅓ years of fighting the poor, little half-country of North Vietnam, victory is not even in sight.

The big question that everybody asks is: *Why* don't we win in Vietnam? We have 500,000 servicemen there, and nightly newscasts tell of battles and bombing raids. Yet, nobody talks of victory, even as an ultimate objective. Secretary McNamara looks into his crystal ball and tells us "we are no longer losing." From U.S. sources in Vietnam emanate gloomy forecasts that the war may last five, ten, or even 15 years.[1]

After two years of continuous bombing, why isn't North Vietnam destroyed? What could be left worth bombing? Americans who know what conventional bombing did to Berlin and Tokyo in World War II simply cannot understand what is the matter. The answer to this question was given in August 1967 by Congressman Gerald Ford. He showed the charts reproduced on the preceding page which prove that the Johnson Administration has secretly handcuffed American pilots by forbidding effective action against important targets. Only 30% of the strategic targets in North Vietnam have ever been hit by a bomb.

American pilots are forbidden to bomb five of North Vietnam's six key industrial targets. More than "100 vital fixed enemy" positions have never been touched. Ford's charts prove that U.S. bombs have *never* hit 90% of North Vietnam's war-making industrial complex, 75% of its air defenses, 75% of its oil storage depots, 75% of its vital transportation network, 67% of its military facilities, and 35% of its power complex. Our pilots are given seven pages of instructions on what they can*not* hit in North Vietnam.[2]

The Pentagon did not dispute any of Congressman Ford's figures. Instead, Secretary McNamara replied that Ford didn't understand the objective of our bombing program.

After studying the Ford charts, it is easy to understand what General John P. McConnell, Chief of Staff of the U.S. Air Force, meant when he said that the war in Vietnam could be won "virtually overnight" if the President would permit the Air Force to do the job.[3]

Bombing is not the whole story. Admiral Roy L. Johnson, when Commander in Chief of the U.S. Pacific Fleet, said that our Seventh Fleet could do the job in a day or two if our Navy were given orders to put a naval quarantine on Haiphong. Yet, the Administration refuses to give this order. The Soviet minister of merchant marine boasted that more than *30 Soviet ships trade each day* with North Vietnam.[4] Our Navy is *not* permitted to stop the constant flow of weapons and supplies— from Communist countries and from our so-called friends—destined to kill American boys.

McNamara's response to those who have pointed out the privileged sanctuaries he has given the Communists is to announce the construction of a wall between North and South Vietnam. As Major General Thomas Lane so aptly pointed out:

> "The Chinese Wall was built to keep out barbarians. The Maginot Line was built to keep out the Germans. It is the persistent illusion of men who have lost the will to fight that bricks and mortar—or electronics—can be substituted for the spirit. Fighting men know better."[5]

Congressional hearings, books, magazines, and newspapers are filled with proof that our commanders could win quickly *if* permitted to do so. High-ranking military authorities have laid out sound, specific plans on how to get the job done. These plans involve using only conventional (nonnuclear weapons. For example, former Chief of Staff of the U.S. Air Force, General Curtis E. LeMay, set forth in *U.S. News & World Report* of October 10, 1966 his views on "How to Win the War in Vietnam." He described in detail how to bring it to a speedy and victorious conclusion. He showed that this would result in the least cost in American lives because "you don't save a dog any pain by cutting off his tail an inch at a time." General LeMay's article is such good common sense that the question cries for an answer: Why doesn't the LBJ Administration follow these sound proposals, or similar ones which have been made? Why do we persist in the "no-win" policy in Vietnam?

On August 9 and 10, 1967 our top U.S. military commander in the Pacific, Admiral Ulysses S. G. Sharp, gave the Senate Preparedness Investigating Subcommittee his prescription for winning in Vietnam. Even though the Pentagon heavily censored his testimony, his formula was clear: close the North Vietnam port of Haiphong with mines, and bomb all the "off limits" military targets in North Vietnam.[6]

The Senators agreed. On September 1, the Senate Preparedness Investigating Subcommittee *unanimously* urged President Johnson to close Haiphong and to strike "all meaningful targets with a military significance." The Senators said this is "the best and very possibly only hope" for a quick and successful end to the conflict.[7]

President Johnson is the one who decides whether targets are on or off limits. Each week, he looks over photos and maps of targets in North Vietnam, and then makes his personal selections.[8] What a way to run a war! Not even Franklin

Roosevelt tried to dictate battle tactics during World War II.

The LBJ Administration is fighting the Vietnam war in the most costly possible way—costly in lives and costly in money. It is also costly in votes.

There have been times when war has reaped political profit for the administration in power, but there is no way that Lyndon Johnson can profit from a prolongation of the war. That was proved by the reverses his Administration suffered in the election of 1966. Johnson's political future depends on ending the war in some way.

There are certainly those around Johnson who are ideologically opposed to defeating Communism anywhere, anytime, whether in Korea, at the Berlin Wall, at the Bay of Pigs, or in Vietnam. But with LBJ in the White House, politics could be expected to override these advisers. The Walt Rostows, the Robert McNamaras, the Paul Nitzes, the Dean Rusks may have their undisclosed motives. But a politician's first law is to get reelected. And Johnson is nothing if he is not a politician. He desperately wants to get rid of the Vietnam war in plenty of time before the 1968 election. His own reelection depends on it. He has tried craven appeasement of Hanoi and Moscow, plus promises of unlimited concessions and handouts, without success.

Why does Johnson refuse to use any of the obvious solutions advocated by his military advisers? What consideration could possibly be more compelling to LBJ than his own reelection? As the Bard said, "Ay, there's the rub."

The Truth Came Out

Dean Rusk let the cat out of the bag one day in September 1966 when he testified before the Senate Preparedness Investigating Subcommittee. Goaded by Senator Strom Thurmond with the question of *why* we are following a "weak-kneed, spineless policy of not winning in Vietnam," Rusk answered with uncharacteristic candor instead of the usual diplomatic doubletalk:

"Senator, we can have a great war any five minutes we want it. . . . We can let this [action in Vietnam] move into a general area that would *knock out 300,000,000 people in the first hour.* . . . The effort has been to take the action necessary to sustain the peace and prevent *a course of aggression from being launched*, and, at the same time, if possible, prevent us all from sliding down the slippery slope into a *general war.*"[9] (emphasis added)

When Rusk talked about knocking out "300,000,000 people in the first hour" in a "general war," there is only one thing he could possibly mean: a nuclear exchange between the Soviet Union and the United States. No other nation has the capability to wage nuclear war and to do that kind of damage. When Rusk talked about preventing "a course of aggression from being launched," there is only one thing he could possibly mean: a nuclear attack on America by the Soviets. It is obvious that we are not going to attack them first.

Therefore, translated from its egghead language, Rusk's statement admits that we dare not win in Vietnam because the Administration is *afraid* that, if we did, the Soviets would launch a nuclear attack on the United States.

Secretary McNamara confirmed this reason when he went before the Senate Preparedness Investigating Subcommittee to answer critics of his bombing policy in Vietnam. On August 25,

1967, in his prepared statement to the Senate, McNamara said:

> "The tragic and long-drawn-out character of that conflict in the South makes very tempting the prospect of replacing it with some new kind of air campaign against the North. But however tempting, such an alternative seems to me completely illusory. To pursue this objective would not only be futile but *would involve risks* to our personnel and *to our nation that I am unable to recommend.*"[10] (emphasis added)

How could an "air campaign" against North Vietnam involve such terrible "risks . . . to our nation"? There is no way North Vietnam can hit the United States. There is no way Red China can hit the United States now—although it may have that capability by 1970. Only the Soviet Union has the present capability of hitting "our nation."

This means that Johnson and McNamara will *not* destroy most of the strategic targets Congressman Ford showed have never been hit, and will *not* put a real blockade on the port of Haiphong—because they are *afraid* of provoking a Soviet nuclear attack against the U.S.

How could the great United States be *afraid* that the Soviets might attack us with nuclear weapons? Only because:

1. We have lost the overwhelming nuclear superiority we had when the Johnson-McNamara Administration took office.

2. We have no way to shoot down Soviet missiles (in other words, we have no anti-missile defense).

In 1961, when President Eisenhower left the White House, the United States had unquestioned military supremacy. We had nuclear superiority over the Soviets of about ten to one. In the last seven years, behind the facade of ever-increasing spending for the war in Vietnam, our nuclear strength has been reducd to the point where the Soviet Union is now blackmailing us into offering up thousands of American boys as hostages and sacrifices in Vietnam in a war they are not permitted to win. If the Soviets can blackmail us into this betrayal of the flower of our youth, they can blackmail us into anything, including the surrender of the United States.

The Schriever Report

On July 12, 1967, front-page headlines across the nation jolted Americans out of their complacent assumption that "there'll always be an America."

SOVIETS TAKING NUCLEAR LEAD
Los Angeles Times

STUDY SAYS SOVIET CUTS MISSILE GAP
The New York Times

SOVIET NUCLEAR LEAD SEEN
Indianapolis Star

'MEGATON GAP' STARTS THIS YEAR
Topeka Daily Capital

U.S. WARNED IT WILL LOSE NUCLEAR
PUNCH TO RUSSIA
St. Louis Globe-Democrat

U.S. FACES NUCLEAR WEAPONS GAP
San Antonio Express

RUSSIA SEEN FORGING AHEAD IN
MISSILE RACE   *San Diego Union*

These and similar front-page headlines heralded a sensational new report entitled *The Changing Strategic Military Balance: U.S.A. vs. U.S.S.R.*, published by the American Security Council. Prepared at the request of the U.S. House Armed Services Committee, this document was immediately issued also as a Committee report, published by the Government Printing Office, dated July 1967. The Report was loaded with statistics to prove the following main points:[11]

1. "The Soviet Union is succeeding in its massive drive toward strategic military superiority, and the United States is cooperating in this effort by slowing down its side of the arms race."

2. The year 1967 is "a crossover period" when the U.S.S.R. nuclear firepower will "equal or exceed the U.S." nuclear firepower.

3. By 1971, "a massive megatonnage gap will have developed" and "the U.S. and the U.S.S.R. will have reversed their roles in a ten-year period."

4. The United States no longer has "a superior position in deliverable strategic weapons. There is still time to regain superiority, but time is on the side of the one which uses it. Because of long lead times for weapon development and production, however, the decision to do so must be made in the year 1967."

The Committee which signed this amazing Report is a who's who of high-ranking military and nuclear authorities:

General Bernard A. Schriever, USAF (Ret.),
    Chairman

General Paul D. Adams, USA (Ret.)

Lieutenant General Edward M. Almond, USA
    (Ret.)

Professor James D. Atkinson

Admiral Robert L. Dennison, USN (Ret.)

Vice Admiral Elton Watters Grenfell, USN (Ret.)

General Curtis E. LeMay, USAF (Ret.)

Admiral Ben Moreell, CEC, USN (Ret.)

Professor Stefan T. Possony

General Thomas S. Power, USAF (Ret.)

Vice Admiral W. A. Schoech, USN (Ret.)

Major General Dale O. Smith, USAF (Ret.)

Admiral Felix B. Stump, USN (Ret.)

Doctor Edward Teller, (Father of the H-Bomb)

Rear Admiral Chester Ward, USN (Ret.)

General Albert C. Wedemeyer, USA (Ret.)

Major General W. A. Worton, USMC (Ret.)

The core of the Schriever Committee Report is the Chart reproduced on the next page entitled "Megatonnage Delivery Capability." "Delivery capability" means how much explosive a nation can hit the enemy with, and "megatonnage" is the way we measure the power of nuclear weapons. "Strategic weapons" are weapons capable of hitting the enemy in his homeland, or of protecting the homeland from attack. The Chart is based on 84 pages of statistics comparing U.S.-U.S.S.R. relative strength in intercontinental ballistic missiles, intermediate and medium range ballistic missiles, anti-ballistic missiles, submarine-launched missiles, strategic bombers, and space weapons.[12]

In 1962, the U.S. had overwhelming superiority over the Soviet Union. In the succeeding years, U.S. nuclear strength has been steadily reduced until today it is only about one-half what it was at the time McNamara became Secretary of Defense. By 1971, under McNamara's announced plans, we will have lost about 90% of our deliverable megatonnage.[13]

Meanwhile, Soviet strength, starting from very little in 1962, has climbed steadily upwards. In 1967, the Soviets *crossed over* and passed the U.S. in megatonnage delivery capability! By 1971, the Soviets will have an overwhelming lead.

Most graphs which show activity over a period of years will have curves and fluctuations. When

MEGATONNAGE DELIVERY CAPABILITY
ALL STRATEGIC WEAPONS

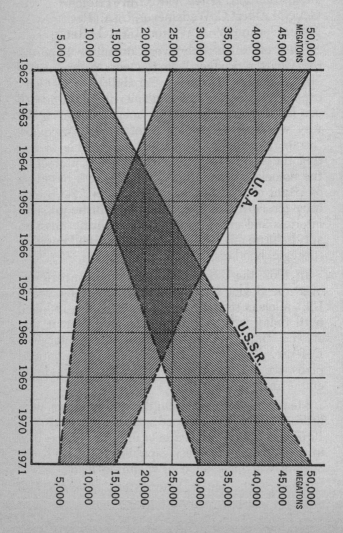

you see a graph where one line goes consistently up, and the other line goes consistently down, you can be sure it wasn't any accident. It was planned that way.

The one arm of the Big X on this chart is the Kremlin's plan for the conquest of the world with nuclear weapons. The other arm of the Big X is the McNamara-Nitze-Gilpatric-Brown-Rostow plan for the nuclear disarmament of the United States. The Big X Chart from 1962 to 1967 shows the *reality* of the disarmament these men have *already* brought about in nuclear weapons—the only weapons which can protect America in the nuclear age. The Big X Chart from 1967 to 1971 shows their plans for the immediate future—plans which must be changed if we are to remain free and independent. The full description of *how* they disarmed us and *why* they disarmed us, is given in *Strike from Space* by Rear Admiral Chester Ward, USN (Ret.), and Phyllis Schlafly (second edition, 1966).

Pentagon Reply

When the sensational Schriever report hit the news on July 12, 1967 reporters immediately rushed over to the Pentagon to obtain the official reply. The Pentagon issued a short, carefully-worded statement which—

1) Did *not* dispute the accuracy of anything in the Schriever report;

2) Did *not* deny that the Soviets are *now* ahead of the U.S. in megatonnage delivery capability;

3) Did *not* deny that by 1971 the Soviets will have a ten-to-one-nuclear lead over the U.S.; but

4) Merely claimed that we have "enough" weapons to "convince" the Soviets they would be foolish to attack.

What if the Soviets are *not* convinced?

The fact is that your life is no longer protected by the overwhelming nuclear strength America had when McNamara took office. It is protected *only* by McNamara's *guess* that the Soviets won't destroy us with a nuclear Pearl Harbor—even though they can. Yet, McNamara is the same Secretary of Defense who was—

1) wrong about the Bay of Pigs in 1961;

2) wrong in thinking that the Soviets would not betray the first nuclear test ban in 1961;

3) wrong in thinking that Khrushchev would not ship missiles into Cuba in 1962;

4) wrong in every major decision about the war in Vietnam, including underestimating the cost in the current year by $20 billion.

When Soviet nuclear power climbs to the top of the Big X, then control of the world will be in the hands of criminal conspirators who look upon Americans exactly as Richard Speck looked upon those eight Chicago nurses before he coolly and sadistically murdered them. It is hard to realize that there are criminals so depraved. But that is what Communism is—Speckism on a worldwide scale. What Speck did with a knife and a rope, the Kremlin bosses desire to do more efficiently and more thoroughly with their big nuclear weapons which McNamara testified have a yield of "about 100 megatons."[14] This is about 10 times greater than our most powerful weapon.

One of the prime purposes of government, according to our Constitution, is to "provide for the common defense." The present Johnson-Humphrey-McNamara Administration has failed in this essential duty—and 1968 gives the voters their *last* chance to remedy the situation.

chapter XI

LEADERSHIP: FOR SURRENDER OR FOR FREEDOM?

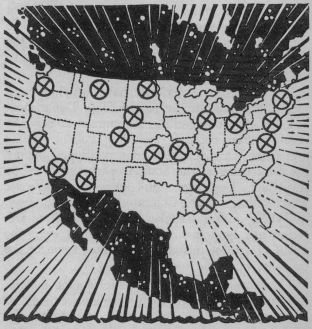

One hot Texas afternoon in August 1966, Charles J. Whitman climbed up into an observation tower at the University of Texas and fired round after round from his rifle at innocent pedestrians below. Before he was finally killed by a policeman, 14 persons had met their death.

The inevitable investigations that followed

turned up some believe-it-or-not facts. About
half the persons killed by Whitman died because
they walked out across the University campus in
range of Whitman's fire after being warned but
refusing to believe that a sniper was really in the
tower. Furthermore, a University psychiatrist revealed that Whitman had told him he planned
to go up into the tower and start shooting people.
The psychiatrist failed to alert anyone.[1]

Our refusal to believe warning signals cannot
save us from danger ahead. We must not be like
those who become so upset by reading about the
bad effects of smoking—that they decide to give
up reading.

For 25 years, Americans have watched with
incredulity and dismay as the State Department
aided and encouraged the Communist takeover of
country after country, including Poland, China,
and Cuba. As each new country slipped behind
the Iron Curtain, the State Department acted so
surprised: "Oops, we didn't know the people we
were aiding were Communists; and anyway,
everybody makes mistakes." But if the State Department's ignorance or incompetence were the
result of honest mistakes, sometime, some of the
mistakes would be in our favor.

The same is true of the McNamara policies
beginning in 1961. As each strategic weapon was
scrapped, cancelled, phased out, or postponed,[2]
McNamara and his egghead entourage presented
Congress with hundreds of pages of doubletalk
about "obsolescence," "cost-effectiveness," "keeping the option," and "assured destruction
capability."

The Big X Chart in the previous Chapter proves
conclusively that there is a plan to disarm the

U.S. of nuclear superiority—and that this plan has resulted in the dramatic, rapid scrapping of U.S. nuclear power—even while the enemy, which has vowed to "bury" us, is expanding his nuclear arsenal as fast as he can. The Big X Chart shows that *all* decisions reduced U.S. nuclear strength, and *no* decisions increased it. Every policy decision spelled weakness, and not a single policy spelled strength. Such a graph could *not* be the result of a series of good-faith decisions or of honest mistakes.

Our present position on the Big X Chart reminds us of the story about the man who fell off the 20th floor of a building. As he passed the sixth floor, a friend shouted: "Mike, so far you're all right."

The lever that has enabled the McNamara clique to accomplish this destruction of our nuclear superiority is the Federal spending power. McNamara wields the greatest concentration of total power ever held by a single man: he has directed the spending of $50 to $70 billion a year for seven years. This power has been used—not to build the defense that our nation needs and must have—but for the benefit of the corrupt Democrat politicians who want to perpetuate themselves in office, and for the ideological purposes of the disarmers who are causing the suicide of the West.

McNamara has used this spending power to build a gigantic machine of payrollers. Almost half of the total civilian employees of the Federal Government are in the Defense Department. McNamara bosses 1,272,555 civilians—not counting *any* of the military. The Defense Department now has more civilian employees than the Post Office Department. In addition, McNamara has used the spending power to build the largest personal staff in the Government. When he took over in 1961, there were about 1,500 employees reporting directly to him. Today there are more than 70,000 employees reporting directly to McNamara. When he took over in 1961, there were 150 persons in the upper pay brackets in the Defense Department; now there are more than 32,000.[3]

What McNamara's use of his spending power has done to the defense of the United States is proved by the Big X Chart. It is proved by his confession on September 18, 1967 that the U.S. no longer has the capability to destroy the Soviet weapons that can destroy us. It is proved by his "no-win" war in Vietnam. It is proved by the way he has blocked all effective action against Castro in Cuba. Our defenses are so weak that we no longer dare to enforce the Monroe Doctrine even in North America.

The TFX contract proves the absolutism of his spending power. The McNamara-Gilpatric-Korth trio was able to override *all* the Air Force and Navy combat experts, *all* the civilian experts, *all* the damaging evidence unfolded in Senate investigations, and give the *largest* contract in history to the *high* bidder with the *poor* product. It was bad enough that McNamara threw away $13 billion on an alleged fighter plane that was no good in the first place and cannot be used as a fighter. It was bad enough that he channelled this money to the political grafters who would use it to get themselves re-elected.

But the TFX is far worse than that because it fits perfectly into the plan for scrapping the nuclear strength of the United States. It means spending enormous sums of money, while giving us no defense. It threw away five years of precious time during which we were *not* building the aircraft, the nuclear weapons, or the anti-missile defenses we need to stay ahead of our enemies.

The Real Purpose Of McNamara's "Thin" Anti-Missile

Officially, the Pentagon was cool about the Schriever Report. But behind this facade, McNamara began making frantic efforts to counter it. Something had to be done, and fast. Too many people and too many Congressmen read the Schriever Report and understood its implications.

Almost as many read the remarkable scenario written by Congressman Craig Hosmer, ranking House Republican on the Joint Congressional Atomic Energy Committee, describing in graphic detail what could happen to America if we rely on McNamara's judgment and it proves wrong again. His map, reproduced at the beginning of this chapter, shows how 17 Soviet super-bombs can destroy U.S. population centers and weapons.

Republicans began to make a major campaign issue out of McNamara's stubborn refusal to build the Nike X anti-missile. On September 14, 1967, former Vice President Richard Nixon issued a strong warning that we must "go ahead at all costs" to build an anti-missile system to counter the growing Soviet ballistic strength and a possible threat from Red China. Nixon went on to show how the phony "missile gap" issue used by Kennedy in the campaign of 1960 can now be turned on the Administration as "a deadly boomerang."[4]

On September 19, 1967, headlines proclaimed that McNamara intends to build a "thin" anti-missile defense to protect our country against Red

China by 1972. Loud hurrahs went up because so many Americans thought this meant that Mc-Namara had, in effect, conceded the foolishness of most of his arguments against the anti-missile for the past several years.

Did this announcement really mean that McNamara had reversed his policies and was now going to start building the defense we need? Not a chance. The liberal press, including *Newsweek, The New York Times,* and the *St. Louis Post-Dispatch,* clearly recognized and stated that the primary purpose of the newly-announced "thin" anti-missile program is *not* to protect us against Red China in 1972—but to protect the Johnson Administration against Republican criticism in 1968. In other words, McNamara's response to the Schriever Report was *political,* and not military at all. By putting up the "thin" Nike X umbrella, he hoped to take the issue out of the 1968 campaign.

This is all made clear in the very speech in which McNamara announced the "thin" anti-missile system: 95% of the speech was devoted to arguments *against* the anti-missile system and to assuring the liberals and the Soviets that he is *not* going to protect American cities against a Soviet missile attack. But why not? The Soviets *today* have the capability of destroying America with nuclear weapons; Red China does not. The U.S. Joint Chiefs of Staff have *unanimously* for three years recommended that we go ahead with a "thick" anti-missile system to protect us against the Soviets. But McNamara still refuses to let us have it.[5]

The most McNamara claims for his new "thin" system is that it may protect us against Red China in 1972. Based on his past record, it is easy to predict that even this "thin" program will be subject to stall, delay, and the usual combination of big spending but no defense.

"Thin" is the right word to describe McNamara's new proposal to build an anti-missile defense against Red China. It is so "thin" that every candidate in 1968 should be able to poke holes in it and make sure the public is not deceived.

McNamara's Mini-MIRVs

The Schriever Report so authoritatively discredited everything McNamara has been saying for seven years about U.S. nuclear superiority that he was forced to create an entirely new "cover" to confuse the public about what he has done to American nuclear strength. He found the perfect answer in the MIRV, which stands for Multiple Individual Reentry Vehicles, and simply means separate warheads on a single missile.

Close investigation shows that the MIRV, instead of being a wonderful new weapon to protect America, is instead another McNamara deception. He plans to take the Minuteman missiles we have, and divide and subdivide the warheads into three to ten MIRVs each. This enables McNamara to razzle-dazzle everybody with a numbers racket. The press gushed forth with the news that the number of our warheads will be fantastically increased from 1,710 to about 7,500. In the hands of inaccurate reporters, McNamara gets even more mileage out of it; many of them are already talking about the staggering number of new *missiles*. This is false; under the MIRV plan, not a single new *missile* will be added.

The truth is that McNamara's Mini-MIRV plan is a clever device for reducing U.S. nuclear firepower even more than he already has. Having scrapped our 24-megaton bomb, having scrapped or scheduled to scrap all our multi-megaton missiles, McNamara has already cut our missile firepower down to the one-megaton range. The MIRV is a device to take us down even lower so that our missile warheads will be only a small fraction of one megaton. The Mini-MIRVs cannot give us as much firepower as the Minuteman warheads they will replace because each MIRV will have to carry its own complex guidance equipment and reentry shield—and this takes weight away from the payload.

Both the MIRV plan to give us multiple mini-warheads, and the 'thin' anti-missile system against Red China, are deceptions like the much-publicized MOL program announced by LBJ in August 1965—and are just as incapable of giving us the defense we need as the flying Edsel. As the 1968 election approaches, we can expect more McNamara publicity stunts designed not for defense —but for political propaganda. Old McNamara defense deceptions never die—as soon as they fade away, they are replaced by new deceptions.

The Racket Called "Trade"

At the same time that Russia and other Communist countries are supplying North Vietnam with the latest weapons and war materials to kill American troops, the Johnson Administration is promoting increased "trade" with the Soviet bloc, even in strategic items. In his "building bridges" speech of October 7, 1966, Johnson announced the removal of export controls on 400 heretofore strategic items, including electronic computers capable of use by the North Vietnamese to shoot down American planes. Johnson's principal foreign policy adviser is Walt Rostow, who was 3 times rejected by the Eisenhower Administration (says Otepka's brief) because of adverse security findings made by the Air Force and the State Department.[6]

If it were trade, that would be bad enough. But Johnson's "building bridges" program is not trade in any sense of the word. It is a racket by which

Communist purchases of desperately-needed U.S. strategic items are financed by various middlemen (to hide the true nature of the transaction), who in turn are financed by the U.S. taxpayers. One of the principal middlemen in this racket is the Export-Import Bank, whose president, Harold F. Linder, contributed $61,300 to the Democrat Party in 1964.[7] LBJ is repaying this largest of all campaign gifts by asking Congress to increase the Export-Import Bank appropriation 50% (from $9 to $13.5 billion of U.S. taxpayers' money).

Only the alertness of Senator Karl Mundt stopped the export by the Johnson Administration to Red Poland of a unique military instrument made only in the U.S. called a Worden gravity meter. Made of quartz fibers, it is the most accurate gravity measuring device in the world, and is used principally to perfect the flight paths of guided missiles.[8]

Republican Party leadership took a firm stand against trade with Communist countries in May 1967 when Senator Everett Dirksen said:

"Is trade so sweet and profits so desirable as to be purchased at the price we now pay in death and agony?"[9]

Unfortunately, Dirksen did not express the views of all prominent Republicans. On January 16, 1967, a front-page story in *The New York Times* announced an "alliance" between a corporation organized by Governor Nelson Rockefeller and a corporation controlled by the Cyrus Eatons "to try to build economic bridges between the free world and Communist Europe." According to *The New York Times*, this will combine the "resources of the Rockefellers" with the "special entree to Soviet-bloc officialdom" resulting from Eaton contacts over the last 15 years.[10] Among the projects planned for the new Rockefeller-Eaton combine are synthetic rubber and aluminum plants for Communist countries.

The Leadership Essential To Win

The times cry out for *political* leaders equal to the twin challenges of Vietnam and nuclear weaponry.

Death is final, and drafted boys should not be

asked to make this ultimate sacrifice unless they are backed up 100% by political leaders with equal courage, and by the best technology our country can provide. As General Dwight E. Beach, commander in chief of the U.S. Army, Pacific, said in July 1967:

> "Once a soldier has been committed to battle by his government he also has some rights. He has a right to expect the support of his people . . . the right to expect the material products and technology of his economy . . . the right to expect the leadership essential to win."[11]

This kind of leadership is obviously not available in the present Administration. McNamara has stacked the upper civilian echelons in the Pentagon so thoroughly that only a complete housecleaning can reverse his disastrous policies. None of McNamara's politically-motivated stopgap announcements can save us. Not even his exit from Washington can save us because, after seven years of power-grabbing and personnel-stacking in the Pentagon, any replacement by the present Administration would be just as bad.

America's position in 1968 was prophetically described by Allen Drury in this great passage from *Advise and Consent*:

> "The United States had gotten herself into a position vis-a-vis the Russians in which the issue was more and more rapidly narrowing down to a choice between fight and die now, or compromise and die later.
>
> "And out of that fearful peril only the most iron-willed and nobly dedicated and supremely unafraid men could lead the nation."

These are the men who must be sought out and elected to high office without delay.

chapter XII

THE PURGE

The leftwing forces—both obvious and hidden—which have been running our country for the last seven years understand and appreciate the importance of *political action.* Their long tentacles reach out in many fields: to "orchestrate" propaganda through the communications media, to indoctrinate youth in our schools and universities, to create a Socialist intellectual climate through tax-exempt foundations, and to bend business into line with Government contracts. But the leftwing forces never, never lose sight of the basic fact of our time (demonstrated by Hitler's rise to control of the German Republic) which is that big power depends on political action.

Robert McNamara's awarding of the TFX contract proves that, in addition to his adept use of power and propaganda weapons to achieve his objectives, he understands the necessity of oiling city and state machines. The success of the Americans for Democratic Action shows that the left-wing liberals know how to follow through with political action for ideological objectives. The left-wing liberals work directly through COPE and the National Committee for an Effective Congress to get out the vote for liberal candidates, especially for Congress.

Likewise the liberals in the Republican party, particularly the little clique called the New York kingmakers, never lose sight of political action to achieve their objectives. These liberals represent only a small minority of the Republican Party. But, powerful in finance and propaganda, and ruthless in tactics, they never relax their political effort to dictate the Republican nominee for President of the United States. The history of what came out of the kingmakers' smoke-filled rooms from 1936 through 1964 is given in *A Choice Not An Echo* by Phyllis Schlafly.

Unfortunately, conservatives have shown no comparable tenacity for political action, or any realization of the vast importance which control of the Republican Party means to the future of America. They worked hard to elect Delegates to the Republican National Convention in 1964, but they largely failed to use the power which was then in their hands to secure the control of the Republican Party organization which their majority warrants and their principles deserve. In many states, the very same Delegates who worked for the nomination of Barry Goldwater with a fervor unmatched in modern politics—sat in Delegates' caucuses and elected National Committeemen and National Committeewomen who were liberals or "moderates."

In San Francisco in 1964, grassroots Republicans were successful in nominating a candidate who was *not* kingmaker-controlled. Then, predictably, the Republican liberals, like spoiled children, took their marbles and went home. Some openly refused to support the Republican nominee for President; others just sat it out and did nothing to help his campaign.

After Senator Goldwater's defeat in November 1964, these same Republican liberals—who had been so flagrantly disloyal to the ticket nominated by the big majority of Republicans—then had the colossal nerve to tell the conservatives to step aside so the minority liberals could remake the Party into their own image and likeness. Their unsportsmanlike attitude was not appreciated by the faithful Republicans who had stuck by the Party through all the years when their candidates were not nominated.

The first conservative scalp collected by the liberals was that of Dean Burch, National Chairman of the Republican Party. Through an alliance of Republican liberals with others who served their own purposes by trading with the liberals, Dean Burch was dumped in January 1965 and replaced by Ray Bliss. This act surrendered control of the titular leadership of the Republican Party, together with the headquarters office, and the money collected in the name of the Republican Party.

The effect on the morale of grassroots Republicans was far more hurtful than the defeat of Goldwater the preceding November. It wasn't that Burch was all that important, but it was the principle of the thing; and conservatives are people of principle. Nearly all conservatives believed then and still believe that the surrender of Burch was a mistake—that, to paraphrase a famous line, it would have been better to have fought and lost, than never to have fought at all.

The election of Bliss was the signal to start a purge of conservatives at every level of Republican politics. Loyal Goldwater supporters were systematically eliminated from the Washington headquarters of the Republican National Committee. This was followed by an attempted purge at every level of the Republican Party, in the state, district and county Republican organizations, and even in some local women's Republican clubs. At the local level, the John Birch Society issue was widely used although, as a political issue, it was as phony as a $3 bill. Anyone who had fervently supported Goldwater was labelled a Bircher and sanctions were imposed.

This purge was pursued by a working alliance between the ideological Republican liberals, the local henchmen who are paid or promised favors by the kingmaker clique, and the political hacks who have learned that the way to get ahead is to play along with the establishment. The success of this purge varied greatly from state to state, and locality to locality. Grassroots Republicans saw what was happening, but they felt isolated, alone, and leaderless. There was no national political organization in which they could coalesce and maintain esprit de corps. Not being machine-

minded politicians, they did not care to work for
control of the Republican Party just for the sake
of control. Many retreated into various educational organizations where the individual is not so
subject to "the slings and arrows of outrageous
fortune."

Target: Republican Women

Within a few months, the purge at the national
level was fairly well complete with one thorny
exception: Phyllis Schlafly, First Vice President of
the National Federation of Republican Women,
who had been unanimously elected at the 1964
Convention in Louisville. Here is a case history of
how the liberals and their allies continued their
purge. The political columnists, Rowland Evans
and Robert Novak, who always seem to have the
inside information on what is happening in liberal
circles, reported on the first of the long series of
secret meetings held by the get-Phyllis cabal.
Their column of July 2, 1965 described how "sad-
faced Party moderates" at a meeting in Washington of the Republican National Committee,

> "huddled in hotel rooms trying to avert a new
> Republican disaster. The disaster: If nature takes
> its course, the National Republican Women's
> Federation will elect as its president Phyllis
> Schlafly—author of the right-wing tract *A Choice
> Not An Echo.*"[1]

Three weeks later, the "sad-faced Party moderates" had apparently worked out their strategy.
Evans and Novak reported:

> "Already some of the Republican Governors here
> are starting a quiet campaign to prevent the auto-
> matic accession of Mrs. Phyllis Schlafly (author of
> *A Choice Not An Echo, The Gravediggers,* and
> other right-wing tracts) to the prominent post of

chairman of the Republican Women's Federation."[2]

It doesn't take any crystal ball to figure out who those Republican Governors were.

During the rest of 1965, the liberal press, fearful that liberal Republicans would drop the ball and fail to come up with a candidate, kept writing articles goading them into action. For example, in October 1965, the *ADA World*, official publication of the Americans for Democratic Action, threw down the gauntlet with as terse an order as politics has ever seen. In personally targeting Phyllis Schlafly, the *ADA World* commanded:

"Out! Out! Damned Spot."

This sample from the *Detroit Free Press* is typical of many other articles during 1965:

"Mrs. Phyllis Schlafly, the stridently conservative author of the 1964 campaign best-seller, *A Choice Not An Echo*, is in line to be elected president of the National Federation of Republican Women. The prospect of her election to the leadership of the GOP's largest women's organization is sending shudders through the bosoms of liberal and moderate Republicans."[3]

The search for a candidate to oppose Phyllis must have been difficult. It apparently became necessary to pass over all the elected officers of the National Federation, all the members of the Executive Committee, and all the elected present and past state presidents, and to select a candidate who had never been elected to any office in the National Federation or even to a full term as president of her own state Federation. The choice was Mrs. Gladys O'Donnell of Long Beach, California. She had endeared herself to the liberals on May 13, 1965 when she launched a false and defamatory attack on Phyllis' book *The Grave-*

diggers. On that date Mrs. O'Donnell tricked the Board of the California Federation of Republican Women into passing a resolution which falsely implied that *The Gravediggers* was somehow involved in an attack on General Eisenhower. The truth is that the *sole* mention of Eisenhower in *The Gravediggers* is to commend him highly for his defense of Quemoy and Matsu against Chinese aggression.[4]

Mrs. O'Donnell then immediately gave her story to the press, which ran a false front-page article reporting that the California Federation had "blistered" Phyllis Schlafly and singled out for "censure" her book *The Gravediggers.*[5]

Ignorance Is Bliss

The initial strategy to defeat Phyllis for president of the NFRW was worked out by September 1965. Conservatives had long suspected who was behind the plan, but the hard evidence was not available until a year and a half later. On March 22, 1967, Mrs. O'Donnell mailed out as part of her campaign literature a news article from her friendly hometown newspaper, which stated:

> "National GOP Chairman Ray C. Bliss is generally credited with manipulating Mrs. Schlafly out of the NFRW presidency last year. . . . The device used was deferral of the scheduled 1966 election to this year."[6]

Bliss never repudiated this mailing of Mrs. O'Donnell, although Phyllis publicly challenged him to do so.[7]

The "device" referred to above was the postponement of the NFRW Biennial Convention in order to give the liberals an extra year to work out strategy and garner votes to defeat Phyllis.

The postponement was accomplished by a double change in the Bylaws voted at a meeting of the NFRW Board of Directors at the New York World's Fair on September 17, 1965. As described by the official NFRW Parliamentarian in a letter dated October 22, 1965:

"The leadership of the Federation . . . suspended the Bylaws, adopted an amendment with a proviso that was known to be illegal and circulated the proposal and the proviso in a most irregular way to the states for ratification. . . . Suspension of the Bylaws unless there is a provision for it *is not in order or legal.* . . . All of my suggestions were rejected, even while admitting that suspension of Bylaws was illegal. . . . Is this the 'Potomac fever' we have heard about?"

In October 1965, Phyllis had a tremendously-successful speaking tour to Republican Women's clubs all over California, drawing crowds up to 2,000. It became perfectly obvious that the California clubs would support Phyllis for Federation president, even if Californian Mrs. O'Donnell were the candidate against her. The establishment deemed it essential, therefore, to change the site of the next Convention from California (where the NFRW Board had voted to hold it[8]) to a location more accessible to the New York liberals. New Convention bids were called for, and Mrs. O'Donnell saw to it that California did not bid.

By George, It Sure Was Rocky

On May 1, 1966, an April interview with Mrs. Elly Petersen, Governor George Romney's State Chairman, was published in the *Grand Rapids Press.* Mrs. Petersen talked too much and revealed more than she intended. After publicly attacking Phyllis, she predicted that the next NFRW Convention would be held in Washington in May

1967. Why Washington? Why in May? By tradition, the Convention alternates east and west of the Mississippi; and it was time to go west. September was *always* the NFRW Convention month. Mrs. Petersen was not a member of the NFRW Board and had no proper way to be privy to confidential advance information.

It turned out that Governor Romney's employee knew more about the site of the Convention than the Executive Committee which subsequently picked the site. On May 2, 1966, the site of the Convention was changed from California to Washington, D.C. The Executive Committee had been handed a form which exaggerated Washington's Sheraton Park Hotel capacity by 33%, and then was told that none of the other bidding cities (Miami, Cincinnati, Kansas City, St. Louis, Portland, Omaha, Hot Springs, Oklahoma City and Honolulu) was "adequate."

As an extra inducement to bring the Convention to Washington, the District of Columbia Federation offered a cash payment of $1,500 to the NFRW, with a promise of "more." Since the D.C. Federation (with only two clubs) was known not to have such an affluent treasury, NFRW president Mrs. Dorothy Elston was asked where the money came from. She replied:

> "Oh, Allie Marriott was the head of the committee that raised that money."

Mrs. Marriott's husband, J. Willard Marriott, is Governor Romney's principal financial backer, and was the host at a meeting held in New York City in the summer of 1967 to start his presidential campaign rolling.

By January 1967, the time had come to open a frontal attack on Phyllis. Mrs. Elston gave two press interviews attempting to bar Phyllis from the presidency of the Federation because of her children. The *St. Louis Post-Dispatch* reported:

"Mrs. Elston says that many otherwise qualified women cannot be considered for president of the Federation because of their responsibilities to husbands and children. She notes that Mrs. Schlafly is married and has six children. . . . Mrs. Elston says, 'You cannot duck the six kids.'"[9]

After Phyllis protested to Mrs. Elston about the impropriety of such remarks, Mrs. Elston the next day gave another press interview in which she repeated the above, and added:

"Mrs. Schlafly must neglect one or the other [her children or the Federation] 'to do it [the Federation presidency] right.'"[10]

The liberal newspaper which published this interview commented editorially:

"It is, then, with little grace, we believe, that Mrs. Dorothy Elston, president of the National Federation of Republican Women, can cite the admirable family of Mrs. Phyllis Schlafly as one reason why strategists might oppose her for the top post. . . . It sounds to us as if someone has the right to call 'foul' in the Republican Party."[11]

The next scene in this drama was New Orleans, January 24 and 25, 1967, where the NFRW Board of Directors met to elect the Nominating Committee. The press reported:

". . . Governor Nelson Rockefeller had eight paid members of his staff working in the Roosevelt Hotel yesterday and last night trying to wrest control of the Nominating Committee from the Schlafly forces. . . . Nelson Rockefeller didn't come to New Orleans, but his brother, Winthrop, newly elected Republican Governor of Arkansas, was conspicuously active this week."[12]

The Nominating Committee was hand-picked in what reporters called the "perfume-filled rooms," and the establishment-approved list was distributed in advance of the meeting. The seven-member Committee included representatives of the two Rockefeller states (New York and Arkansas) plus Mrs. O'Donnell's closest ally—but no Schlafly supporter.

The Washington Apartment

Shortly after this meeting, the Nominating Committee sent to every club in the United States an official notice regarding the forthcoming election which stated:

"The president must be willing to reside in the Federation apartment in Washington, D.C."[13]

In subsequent letters, Mrs. Elston claimed that this was some new "rule" of the Federation. The fact is there *never* was any such rule binding on the Federation, and the Federation does *not* even have an apartment in Washington. The Federation merely pays the rent on an apartment which Mrs. Elston selected and lives in.

The immediate purpose, of course, was to give the false impression that this "rule" barred Phyllis from the presidency, because everyone knew she could not put her six children in a one-bedroom apartment. But this statement, combined with the direct assault on Phyllis because of her children, had two additional purposes:

1) To discourage the mothers of young children by telling them bluntly they could be the peons in the precincts, but were barred from the highest office in the Federation. Obviously, no normal happily-married woman with children could live in the one-bedroom Washington apartment. One of the wonderful things that happened to the Republican Party in 1964 was the great influx of young mothers who are willing to work for the

Republican Party because they are concerned about what kind of America their children will inherit. These political volunteers are not subject to establishment control because they work from dedication and not for favors.

2) To make sure that the Federation would continue to be controlled from the office of the Republican National Committee. The Federation has a cubbyhole office in the very middle of Ray Bliss's headquarters, where every phone call can be monitored, every visitor observed, and where all NFRW mailings are supervised.

The chairman of the Nominating Committee soon gave an interview to her homestate newspaper, the *Denver Post*, in which she predicted that the Nominating Committee would present a slate of women who are "moderately progressive."[14] The meaning was clear. The Nominating Committee did not even nominate Phyllis for another term as First Vice President despite the thousand letters it received in her behalf. It surprised no one when the Nominating Committee on March 8, 1967 announced that it had chosen Gladys O'Donnell.

The NFRW office, financed by dues from *all* the clubs, immediately began to be used as a campaign headquarters for Mrs. O'Donnell. Mailings favorable to Mrs. O'Donnell and derogatory to Mrs. Schlafly were sent out of this office by the NFRW staff.[15] Mrs. Elston continued her intemperate attacks in the press and on March 23, 1967 even blamed Phyllis for the

> "cockroaches that have recently appeared because we've all been working 12 and 14 hours a day and eating at our desks dealing with the fuss that she [Mrs. Schlafly] has stirred up around the country."[16]

On March 27, 1967 Senator Barry Goldwater wrote a letter to Mrs. Elston proclaiming his neutrality in the contest, and saying complimentary things about both candidates. Mrs. Elston then released to the press only selected portions of the Goldwater letter favorable to Mrs. O'Donnell, while suppressing paragraphs favorable to Phyllis. Apparently Mrs. Elston did not know that Senator Goldwater had sent Phyllis a copy of his letter. When the press phoned Phyllis for comment, she released the remainder of the letter. Reporters then hurried back to Mrs. Elston, who lamely confessed that the missing paragraphs had been deleted by her. She explained that she had censored the parts helpful to Mrs. Schlafly, especially the last paragraph, because, Mrs. Elston said:

"I do not agree with it."[17]

Mrs. O'Donnell then mailed to every club in the country what falsely purported to be the complete Goldwater letter, including a facsimile of his signature, but which omitted this paragraph favorable to Phyllis.

Credentials Chicanery

The voting body for the Convention consisted of one delegate for each of the 4,224 clubs, plus 351 delegates-at-large, plus the National Board. In order to vote, each club delegate was supposed to present the yellow credentials form signed by her club president and countersigned by her club treasurer. These yellow slips were plainly printed in large letters:

"It is necessary to show this credential in order to vote."

As the Convention time approached, the liberals realized that, despite the steady stream of attacks on Phyllis which had poured forth from the NFRW office, they still did not have enough delegates with yellow forms. Moving the Convention site from California to Washington, D.C. to accommodate the New York liberals had given them at least a 1,000-vote advantage because so many conservatives from the more distant states could not afford to attend. Even so, there still were not enough local club presidents sufficiently liberal or sufficiently interested to attend the Convention. So, in the last couple of weeks, a bold new strategy was devised to stop Phyllis.

The new strategy was to ditch the yellow credentials forms altogether and substitute badges issued solely by the state presidents. This enabled the state presidents of New York, Pennsylvania, New Jersey, Michigan and Arkansas to give voters' badges to anyone of their own choosing, without any check whatsoever on whether they were proper delegates. This device enabled women to vote who were not members of the Federation and who did not belong to the clubs they were listed as representing. It enabled state or Party payrollers to be converted into "instant" delegates. It enabled women to vote under false names, and there was even no guarantee against one woman voting twice with different badges.

Getting rid of the yellow credentials form enabled these five states, by fair means or foul, to send 10 to 30 times as many delegates as ever attended a previous Convention. The Arkansas representation, for example, increased from 12 to 100 voting delegates. Governor Winthrop Rockefeller later admitted that Arkansas backed Mrs. O'Donnell "because she was a moderate."[18] The packed delegations from these five liberal-controlled states provided *well over half* of all the votes against Phyllis.

The so-called Credentials Committee was put under the chairmanship of a woman who had been sending out telegrams signing herself as O'Donnell campaign chairman for the state of Virginia. This Committee was given jurisdiction *only* over contested delegates. On the flimsiest and most lint-picking technicalities, more than 100 Schlafly delegates were made to stand as long as 14 hours in hot, dark, crowded corridors waiting to be heard by the Credentials Committee. After the farce of a hearing, nearly all were thrown out. The only rule that seemed to be followed was: If the state president was for O'Donnell, then "we must take the word of the state president"; if the state president was for Schlafly, then dig up some technicality to throw out the delegate, even though she had her yellow credentials form duly signed by her club president and treasurer.

The result was a strange double standard. Eleven Missouri clubs were denied the right to vote because (through no fault of their own) their state treasurer was *one* day late in forwarding dues to Washington. (This state treasurer later told friends that Mrs. Elston had telephoned her from Washington and told her *not* to send in the dues of the 11 clubs because they were chartered in 1967. This was 100% contrary to the ruling published in the December 1966 NFRW newsletter and applied to every other state.)

On the other hand, 743 New York and Pennsylvania delegates were allowed to vote although their states paid only about half the dues since the last Convention (1964), required by the NFRW Bylaws.[19] The official NFRW Statistical

Reports state that the New York membership is 65,000, but New York paid on only 32,500 in 1965, on 35,000 in 1966, and on 46,753 in 1967. NFRW Statistical Reports state that Pennsylvania made a token payment on only 10,734 in 1965, on 14,453 in 1966, and on 45,024 in 1967. In other words, the big states of New York and Pennsylvania were allowed to vote although they were in violation of the Bylaws which require that only clubs "whose dues are paid in full . . . shall be entitled to representation at the Convention."

One member of the Credentials Committee resigned in protest because of the steady stream of biased decisions, but her microphone was cut off when she tried to present her minority report to the Convention.

The Filibuster

The Convention opened on the morning of Friday May 5, with the Invocation and the Star Spangled Banner forgotten, but with Romney campaign literature conspicious on the chairs. With the credentials shenanigans described above, it became imperative to prevent a credentials report from coming before the delegates. The original agenda had *not* even listed a credentials report at the first session. When it was pointed out to Mrs. Elston by a former Congresswoman that the first order of business at every Convention must be the report of the Credentials Committee, then it was scheduled.

A new device had to be found to evade this primary obligation of parliamentary procedure. The Credentials Committee chairman came to the microphone and began to read a report which had just been handed to her. By the time she reached Hawaii (reading the states alphabetically), it was apparent to the entire Convention that her figures were so obviously false that the reading could not be continued. She retired in confusion with Mrs. Elston promising she would be heard later.

Repeated requests for the Credentials Committee report were made by delegates. Each time a delegate called for the Credentials Committee report, she had her microphone cut off, was ruled out of order by the chair, or was silenced by the parliamentarian who kept reading a cropped excerpt from *another* book on parliamentary law which was misleading, out of context, and totally irrelevant because Article X of the NFRW Bylaws states that *Robert's Rules of Order, Revised* shall govern in all matters not covered in the Bylaws.

Robert's Rules of Order, Revised, which NFRW Bylaws state is the final authority, require that the report of the Credentials Committee be given

> "as soon as the opening exercises are concluded, so that it may be known who are entitled to vote. . . . A motion should be made to accept or adopt the report, which . . . is open to debate and amendment."

These rules were *not* complied with at the NFRW Convention. Delegates were *never* given any report of the Credentials Committee as required by *Robert's Rules of Order, Revised.* There was *never* any official determination of who were entitled to vote. Delegates were *refused* their right to debate and vote on any Credentials Committee report. Therefore, under NFRW Bylaws and *Robert's Rules of Order, Revised,* the Convention was illegal.

"Filibuster" is the best word to describe the Convention management. Two days of sessions were planned with two principal objectives: (1)

there would be only a few minutes of time for the business of the Convention, and (2) there would be no possiblity of communication among the delegates themselves. The first day was filled with 30 "unity" speeches which occupied all the time from morning, through a box lunch served in the Convention hall, until after midnight.

Delegates who wanted to participate in the business of the Convention were accused of insulting the Congressmen who were guest speakers. Floor debate was cut short by such subterfuges as presenting the Texas Southern University Choir; it was implied that any delegate who wanted to continue with the business of the Convention must be anti-Negro. Although the principal business before the Convention was the election of the new president, the delegates were refused the right to hear either candidate speak.

The Filibuster also operated to prevent communication among the delegates. Although Mrs. O'Donnell was from California, the largest California delegation in the history of Republican politics had traveled to Washington in support of Phyllis by a margin of three to one. Every precaution was taken to prevent California delegates from socializing with the other states and explaining why.

The policing of the Convention floor to prevent communication among Schlafly delegates was carried out with the precision of a gestapo. The guards, instead of being Federation members, were uniformed men, some of them armed, who thoroughly intimidated the women. The president of the Southern Division of the California Federation, representing 40,000 women, could not walk down the aisle to speak to members of her delegation without being harassed and threatened by male guards.

Mrs. Elston finally admitted weeks later that "15 members of the Republican National Committee staff were permitted to provide technical assistance" to the NFRW Convention.[20] The fact is that all Ray Bliss's employees were working at the Convention; the National Committee headquarters was locked and the switchboard closed.

One of the pieces of "technical assistance" that the Republican National Committee provided was technical assistance to shut off the microphones in the areas of the Schlafly delegations, but turn them on in the areas of the O'Donnell delegations. According to Drew Pearson, who published what he said was a confidential memorandum of instructions Mrs. O'Donnell gave to her key workers, the microphones were handled by Jim Baker, one of Bliss's personal assistants.[21] While feigning "neutrality," Ray Bliss later confirmed that Jim Baker "helped set up some of the physical arrangements."[22] The handling of the microphones was one of the most flagrantly biased aspects of the whole Convention. One of the few Schlafly delegates who successfully addressed the Convention achieved her objective solely because she had the foresight to go to the microphone in the New York delegation.

Another piece of "technical assistance" was the finagling of the seating arrangement. It was not in alphabetical order. Michigan, New York and Pennsylvania were placed together in the front rows under the television lights, while the Schlafly delegations were scattered in the poorly-lighted rear of the hall and on the outer fringes, scarcely visible or audible to the platform and press. Anyone who tends to doubt the existence of the liberal establishment should have attended the NFRW Convention. There it was plain to see, in all its geographic clarity—making the appropriate noises on cue, indulging in the ultimate in mob rudeness when they booed the two very distinguished Republican women who seconded Phyllis' nomination.

On The Day Of The Voting

After weeks of evasion about election procedure, Mrs. Elston finally promised in writing that Phyllis' representatives would be permitted to observe the preparation and sealing of the voting machines, and to participate in the security guarding of the machines until the polls opened. These promises were nationally reported by the press.[23]

When it became known that Phyllis' representatives were two of the most experienced ballot security men in the United States, Richard H. Carpenter and John D. Lewis of Phoenix, Arizona, Mrs. Elston reneged on her written promises. Formal protests to the legality of the election were presented to Mrs. Elston by Mr. Carpenter and Mr. Lewis *before* the polls opened, and to the Convention body by Mrs. Rosalind Frame, delegate from Georgia, *before* the polls closed—in both cases *before* the results were known. Here is the original signed protest:

"To Whom It May Concern:

"I hereby formally protest the election for President of the National Federation of Republican Women held on May 6, 1967 for the following reasons:

"1) The representatives of Phyllis Schlafly were not given notice of the preparation of the voting machines as promised by the President of the Federation in her letter to Mrs. Robert Hoffman,

Campaign Manager for Phyllis Schlafly, dated May 4, 1967;

"2) The representatives of Phyllis Schlafly were not allowed to observe the preparation of the voting machines for voting as promised by the President of the Federation in the letter referred to above;

"3) The representatives of Phyllis Schlafly were denied the right to participate in the security guarding of the voting machines from the time they were prepared for voting until the polls opened as promised by the President of the Federation in the letter mentioned above;

"4) No test voting was allowed.

"Because of the above, the traditional American safeguards of proper checks and balances have not been preserved. . . .

"Therefore, the election should be declared void. Dated this 6th day of May, 1967.

(Signed) Richard H. Carpenter
(Signed) John D. Lewis"

Soon after the opening of the polls on Saturday morning, May 6, began the incredible harassment of the Ohio delegation, which was the largest single delegation supporting Phyllis. Women were forced to stand in lines up to three hours waiting for their names to be found on the list. It is too much to believe that this harassment could have been anything except a tactic to stall and harass in the hope that many Schlafly delegates would give up and leave without voting.

By contrast, in mid-morning several hours after the voting had begun, busloads of women began to arrive direct from New York, Pennsylvania, New Jersey and Michigan. These women had never been on the Convention floor, and were brought in solely to vote against Phyllis. They came into the hotel, were taken directly to their state headquarters where they were given quickie credentialling and instructed how to vote, then to the voting area, and then back home on the busses. Interviewed in the lobby, many could not give the names of the Federation candidates, or the names of the clubs they were supposed to be representing. Many admitted that they were given the free bus ride and free meals.

Robert's Rules of Order, Revised states that no one can be on the list of voters "who has not registered as present." The NFRW Bylaws state that the list of voters must be provided two hours before the polls open.[24] Therefore, all the "voters" who were bussed in after the polls opened on Saturday were illegal. They had no credential forms signed by their club presidents. They just had a badge hung on them, and they voted. Mrs. Elston admitted that six busloads came in on Saturday; eight were seen and interviewed. Some busses arrived as late as five hours after voting had begun. In the words of one stanza of the poem written by Phyllis' son, John, which was thought worthy of publication by the *Los Angeles Times*:[25]

"On the day of the voting there came
Big busses of ignorant dames;
    Encouraged by doles,
    They were sent to the polls,
Then left, while the righteous cried, 'Shame!'"

Immediately following the Convention, Phyllis requested permission to inspect the voters' signature lists, a basic right not only of every candidate, but of every voter. Mrs. Elston sent a wire which said: "Request denied. The Convention has spoken."[26] What was she hiding? The answer is obvious: (1) the identities of the women who were bussed in, and (2) the actual count of the women who voted. All we know is how many votes were

recorded on the machines; we do not know how
many actually voted.

After the Convention, four delegates filed a
formal protest with Chairman Ray Bliss stating:

"The undersigned women, who served as delegates to the Convention of the National Federation of Republican Women in Washington, D.C.
on May 5-6, formally protest the gross illegalities
and irregularities which characterized both the
Convention proceedings and the election. We believe that these irregularities defeated the choice
of the majority of the delegates and members of
the Federation. . . . What is at stake here is the
integrity of the ballot. In our opinion this was a
controlled and rigged election which has constituted an election fraud depriving the half million
Federated Republican women of their representation at the National Convention."

On May 10, 1967, this protest was put into the
Congressional Record by Congressman John Ash-
brook who included these words of his own:

"Mr. Speaker, I had a firsthand opportunity to
observe the conduct of the Biennial Convention
of the National Federation of Republican Women
which was held in Washington during last week.
I know when I see a railroad running through the
middle of a house so it was not hard to observe
what was transpiring. . . . If Mrs. Schlafly wants
to support those who stacked the deck against her,
it would be sheer grace on her part. On the
other hand, it is clear to me that those who
manipulated, gave unfair rulings and engaged in
unfair tactics have no right whatsoever to ask for
unity. They were the most divisive force I have
ever seen in the Republican Party—the same
dominant elements we saw playing the spoiler's
role in 1964."

The behind-the-scenes forces which directed the
campaign against Phyllis were not only the lib-

erals. They were joined by all those who feel it is to their own interests to keep Republican women neutralized. The Republican Party is carried on the shoulders of the women who do the work in the precincts, ringing doorbells, distributing literature, and doing all the tiresome, repetitious campaign tasks. Many men in the Party frankly want to keep the women doing the menial work, while the selection of candidates and the policy decisions are taken care of by the men in the smoke-filled rooms. All those building their own political machine want only machine-people who can be controlled. In Phyllis, they recognized one who could not be neutralized or silenced, and who would fight for women to express their ideals in matters of policies and candidates commensurate with the work the women do for the Party. On the other hand, the press reported that:

"Mrs. O'Donnell admitted freely that one of her reasons for campaigning to prevent conservative Phyllis Schlafly of Alton, Illinois from moving into the Federation presidency was that Mrs. O'Donnell wants to 'neutralize' the women's national group."[27]

In addition, once it became clear that the liberal establishment would put enough money and influence into the NFRW election to swing it, while the more numerous conservative men sat on the sidelines, the opportunists came out of the woodwork and joined what they thought was the winning side. They hoped this would enable them to sell their services to any well-heeled liberal Republican presidential candidate.

"Victors In Defeat"

The vote was announced on Saturday afternoon as 1,910 for Gladys O'Donnell and 1,494 for Phyllis Schlafly. After shaking hands with Mrs. O'Donnell,

Phyllis went immediately to another large room in the Sheraton Park for her first opportunity to speak with the more than 2,500 delegates, alternates and other friends who had traveled to Washington in her support. The press reported that they "looked like victors in defeat."

The first moral of the NFRW Convention is that the objective of the liberal establishment is not "unity" but rule or ruin. Conservatives have never tried to purge liberals, but have supported all Republicans who by service and seniority are entitled to high positions. The New York and Michigan liberals, on the other hand, do not believe that conservative Republicans are entitled to any Party position of importance, regardless of their qualifications and record. This was shown in 1964 and proved again in May 1967.

The second moral of the NFRW Convention is that the liberal establishment is not restrained by Robert's Rules of Order, the Marquis of Queensberry Rules for a fair fight, the Golden Rule, or the Eleventh Commandment. As a distinguished Republican Congressman described the NFRW Convention: "They overstole it." They could not conceal all their dishonest tactics.

The "victors in defeat" knew they had participated in a fight worth making. They demonstrated that, despite every pressure and trick, thousands of Republican women's clubs will work and sacrifice for principles of morality and patriotism. These gallant women recognized that the 1967 NFRW Convention was a window through which they could look to the Republican National Convention in 1968. They went home with renewed vigor to work to make sure Republicans have the right candidates in 1968.

chapter **XIII**

DON'T LEAVE POLITICS TO THE POLITICIANS

1968 is *the* year—the most important year of our lives. It is the year when we *must*—

1) Restore law and order to our cities.

2) Win the "no-win" war in Vietnam which has killed or wounded 100,000 American boys—and end the policies which bring on more Vietnams.

3) Clean up the rampant corruption in Washington: the blackmail, bribery and payoffs, the

coddling of security risks and of slick influence-peddlers who enrich themselves at the taxpayers' expense.

4) Protect our homes from a missile attack—and from the suicidal appeasement policies which are disarming America of our once-great nuclear strength.

5) Restore local self-government to our people and reverse the rush of power into the hands of the politicians in Washington. If they cannot make the streets of our nation's capital safe for our citizens, they certainly are not competent to direct our schools, welfare, and urban affairs.

The best practical way to accomplish these objectives is through candidates elected on the ticket of the Republican Party. The overwhelming majority of Republicans would work their hearts out for candidates who promised to fulfill these objectives. These candidates would win in 1968 because the American people are fed up with the moral sickness and the vacuum of leadership they have witnessed in the last seven years. Our task should be easy.

But it isn't. The leftwing pundits and the opportunistic politicians are full of advice for Republicans and whom they should nominate. We are told we must have "moderate" candidates. What does this mean? Is it "moderate" to think racial rioting is "a sign of progress"? Is it "moderate" to promote LBJ's program for trade with Communist countries which in turn are shipping weapons and materials to kill American boys? Is it "moderate" to be imbued with such fuzzy sentimentality toward criminals that our cities are no longer safe? Is it "moderate" to be silent about the McNamara policies which are scrapping our nuclear strength? There is absolutely no reason why the majority of Republicans, who do not believe such things, should accept such candidates.

We are told that Republicans must win at any price, and that the price of victory in 1968 is "unity" under a "moderate," or possibly a compromise ticket that throws the Vice Presidency to a conservative. In October 1967, Republican kingmakers were hedging their bets by holding secret meetings to consider a publicity buildup for a *Democrat* for the Republican nomination for President! He is retired General James Gavin, who recently resigned from the Massachusetts Democratic Advisory Council because LBJ's views are not far enough to the left.

One of the favorite slogans of the liberals is "U for Unity must precede V for Victory." Those who play this game forget that U and V are both preceded by P for Principle. The Republican Party must offer candidates who have strong moral and patriotic principles. *If our leaders don't stand for something, they will fall for anything.*

Those who don't stand for Patrick Henry's stirring cry, "Give me liberty or give me death," fall for the plea of the handout hunter, "Gimme, gimme, gimme." Those who don't stand for the kind of patriotism Nathan Hale made famous in his words, "I only regret I have but one life to give for my country," fall for the slogan "Rather Red than dead." Those who don't stand for the principle of "Millions for defense, but not one cent for tribute," fall for the Great Society giveaways based on billions for payoffs, but cut back on defense. Those who don't stand for MacArthur's great advice, "There is no substitute for victory," fall for the lure of 'building bridges to

Communist countries" while they kill our best young men. Political leaders who don't stand for principle are as ideologically vulnerable as the college beatniks who, because they don't stand for anything, fall for all the four-letter words except soap and bath.

The favorite joke around Washington in 1967 was about a new bill signed by President Johnson. It is a law to require every new automobile to have automatic transmission. The reason for this law is that, in the Great Society, no one is going to be permitted to shift for himself.

"Making Things Happen"

There was once a famous man who said that there are really only three classes of people in the world: a very small elite group which *makes* things happen, a somewhat larger group which *watches* things happen, and a great multitude which *never knows* what happened. Over the last decade, many thousands of concerned Americans have acquired a good understanding of the various forces at work in our nation and are now in the group which watches things happen.

The *only* way you can join the elite group which *makes* things happen is to plunge into political action. Americans can think up a thousand excuses for avoiding political action. They say it is "controversial" and will "hurt business." It is a good thing that the Founding Fathers were not afraid to be controversial, or the famous words of Thomas Jefferson might have been written this way:

"And for the support of this Declaration, with a *moderate* reliance on the protection of Divine Providence, we mutually pledge to each other one hour a week of our lives, $5 a month of our fortunes, and a little of our sacred honor, provided it doesn't hurt business."

As 1967 drew to a close, many grassroots Republicans unfortunately were sitting on the sidelines with the attitude: "I'll wait and see who the presidential candidate is before I work for the Republican Party." This attitude is doomed to failure and frustration because it tries to put the cart before the horse. If informed, dedicated Americans would get out of their non-political easy chairs and join in active participation within the Republican Party, they could have any candidate they want for any office.

There are many devoted Republican volunteers who have worked faithfully since 1964, doing all the precinct drudgery. But the politicians have fed the absurd line to these Republican volunteers that they are bound to work for anyone who gets the Republican nomination, but should have no share in the choosing of the nominees. This leaves the power to choose candidates and determine policies in the hands of the Party payrollers and the political technicians.

This system is all wrong and it makes second-class citizens out of the most faithful Republican workers. The Republican Party belongs just as much, and probably more, to the dedicated volunteers who do the work in the precincts. They are the ones who should pick the nominees and determine the policies. To paraphrase a famous saying: Politics is too important to be left to the politicians.

Leaving politics to the politicians results in situations such as occurred in Rhode Island in March 1967 when there was a special election to fill a vacant House seat. The so-called "Republican" candidate ran on a platform calling for U.S.

withdrawal from Vietnam, abolition of the House Committee on Un-American Activities, and a raft of other leftwing proposals supported only by the most extreme Democrats. The candidate, James Di Prete had publicly supported Lyndon Johnson and had even gone so far as to call Barry Goldwater a "Fascist." Incredible as it may seem, the Republican Congressional Campaign Committee poured $10,000 into Di Prete's campaign. Fortunately, he lost.

When a reporter for the *Washington Post* inquired about the financial support given Di Prete, a spokesman for the Republican Campaign Committee said: "We don't care whether he is a hawk or a dove or a goose, all we care about is winning."

Republican volunteers do care. They are not willing to spend their time and money and effort in order to send a flock of geese to Congress. It is the Republican volunteers, working for patriotism and not payola, who must provide the moral and ideological substance to the Republican Party.

A special study made by the American Conservative Union provides the facts and figures on the "geese" we currently have in Congress. This study proves how 24 of the principal bills of the Kennedy-Johnson Administrations passed *only* because liberal Republicans provided the Democrats with their margin of victory.[1] Those who want to reverse the Johnson policies must realize that our major obstacle is the Republican liberals who vote *against* traditional Republican principles.

It's Up To You

Only one thing will determine who will be the next Republican nominee for President—the votes of some 1,300 Delegates who will attend the Republican National Convention in Miami in August 1968. **You** have a personal responsibility for the votes of the two Delegates from your District.

Will your Delegates be men who can be bought, bribed or blackmailed? Will they be political contortionists, sitting on the fence while they keep their ears to the ground? Will they be men who don't own their own votes, but who are placed in that spot to do as they are told?

Or will your Delegates be men and women who can resist the propaganda and the pressures, and nominate a candidate who will stop coddling criminals and subversives, give us victory over Communism at home and abroad, restore America to its position of military supremacy, cut the Federal spending which is fueling the corruption in Washington, and tell people to stand on their own two feet and stop looking for a Government handout?

The times require that **you** go to work to build the political strength in your district so that those who believe in traditional Republican principles can speak for the Republican Party in its hour of decision. Delegates are chosen by a tremendously complicated procedure, different in every state. But one thing is sure. The only way you can be a Delegate, or be in a position to influence the choice of your Delegates, is as a result of long hours, weeks, and months of service to the Republican Party.

The same is true when it comes to selecting candidates for Congress, Governor, and all the other offices. It is not enough to have the issues on our side; it is not even enough to have attractive and high-principled candidates. It is also necessary to have the base of political power at every level of the Republican Party.

The decision to go into politics is not an easy one. It makes you "controversial" and subjects you to financial and social pressures. It is terribly time-consuming. It is a challenge for patriots of the highest order, who have courage in crisis and controversy, and courage to persevere in the face of discouragements. It is much pleasanter to stay in your comfortable home, writing letters and mailing out literature, feeling that you are doing enough to save America. But that is not enough. Politics is the key to whether we can continue to survive as a free and independent nation.

Nor is it enough that you work only for Delegates. You must work to build strength in the Republican Party so that the traditional principles rank-and-file members believe in, cannot be diluted by the payrollers and opportunists. Work your way up in your precinct, county, district, and state Republican organization. This is the legally-constituted spokesman for the Republican Party in your state, and this is where we need the loud, clear voice of the volunteers. It is wrong for the volunteers to abdicate all the power to those who are seeking some political favor.

Volunteer Republican organizations can play a determining role. They can take the lead in speaking out for traditional Republican principles on so-called "controversial" issues, in selecting nominees, and in publishing voting records of elected officials. California's volunteer organizations, UROC and CRA, are two of the principal reasons behind the election of Ronald Reagan as Governor.

Ballot security should be one of the most urgent objectives to which patriots should turn their attention. Some people have the idea that voting machines guarantee honest elections. Anyone who thinks that voting machines cannot be dishonestly "fixed" must have never heard of slot machines— which, as nearly everyone knows, can be fixed to give the "house" any percentage of the money. Likewise, voting machines can be fixed to give the machine candidate any percentage of the vote.

Most important, the widespread use of election machines opens up the possibility of stealing a national election. Stealing a national election by paper ballots is too immense a task; and anyway, there are not that many crooks in the United States. With voting machines, however, a few crooks in strategic locations can steal millions of votes. The Honest Ballot Association estimates that at least 4,000,000 fraudulent or invalid ballots were cast and counted in the presidential election of 1964. Many elections have been won by much smaller margins.

Even if we nominate the best presidential candidate on the Republican ticket, and even if we have enough votes to elect him, we face the real possibility that election frauds will cheat us of victory. It will take many months of study and planning by dedicated political-action teams in every community to prepare for an honest election in 1968.[2]

On his way to Washington to assume the Presidency in 1861, Abraham Lincoln gave us this sound political advice, still as timely as when he said it:

"I appeal to you to constantly bear in mind that not with politicians, not with presidents, not with office-seekers but with **you** is the question: shall the Union and shall the liberties of this country be preserved to the latest generations."

REFERENCES

I. What the Politicians Won't Tell

1. *U.S. News & World Report,* Aug. 21, 1967, p. 12; Aug. 28, 1967, pp. 49-50; Sept. 25, 1967, pp. 41-43.

II. Riots Secretly Subsidized

1. For background on OEO, see generally, Newman and Wenger, *Pass the Poverty Please,* 1966.
2. *The New York Times,* Aug. 4, 1967; *U.S. News & World Report,* Aug. 14, 1967, p. 27, and Aug. 21, 1967, pp. 66-67.
3. *The New York Times,* Aug. 5, 1967.
4. *The New York Times,* Aug. 9, 1967.
5. Spina telegram, as made public by Senator Winston Prouty.
6. *Chicago Tribune,* Aug. 15, 1967.
7. *The New York Times,* Aug. 8, 1967.
8. *Chicago Tribune,* Aug. 16, 1967.
9. *Barron's,* July 31, 1967.
10. AP Dispatch, Aug. 5, 1967.
11. *Chicago Tribune,* Aug. 10, 1967.
12. Robert S. Allen, Syndicated Column, July 1967.
13. *U.S. News & World Report,* Aug. 14, 1967, p. 42.
14. *Houston Tribune,* Aug. 17, 1967.
15. *U.S. News & World Report,* Aug. 28, 1967, p. 52.
16. *Barron's,* July 31, 1967.
17. Robert S. Allen, Syndicated Column, July 1967.
18. *The New York Times,* July 28, 1967, p. 1.
19. *Barron's,* July 31, 1967.
20. *Chicago Tribune,* Aug. 10, 1967.
21. *Barron's,* July 31, 1967.
22. *St. Louis Post-Dispatch,* Aug. 13, 1967.
23. In *Pennsylvania v. Nelson* (1956), the Supreme Court ruled that the sedition law of Pennsylvania could not be enforced against Nelson, alias Mesarosh, a Soviet spy who helped to steal our atomic secrets.
24. Allen-Scott Syndicated Column, Aug. 1967.
25. *The New York Times,* Sept. 28, 1967.
26. Hall Syndicate, Aug. 1967.
27. *The New York Times,* July 14, 1967.
28. *New York Times* News Service, July 25, 1967.

III. Riots Don't Just Happen

1. NANA, Aug. 9, 1967.
2. *U.S. News & World Report,* Aug. 14, 1967, p. 25.

3. *Life,* July 28, 1967, pp. 27-28.
4. NANA, Aug. 11, 1967.
5. *The New York Times,* Aug. 31, 1967.
6. *U.S. News & World Report,* Sept. 11, 1967, p. 15.
7. *The New York Times,* Sept. 28, 1967.
8. *Washington Post* News Service, Aug. 4, 1967.
9. *Chicago Tribune,* Aug. 5, 1967.
10. *Washington Post* News Service, Aug. 4, 1967.
11. *The New York Times,* Sept. 16, 1967.
12. Allen-Scott Syndicated Column, July 1967.
13. Reprinted in Phillip Abbott Luce, *Road to Revolution,* 1967, p. 117.
14. *Chicago Tribune,* July 30, 1967, p. 14.
15. Ibid.
16. *St. Louis Post-Dispatch,* Feb. 19, 1967.
17. *St. Louis Globe-Democrat,* Aug. 3, 1967.
18. *Chicago Tribune,* July 30, 1967, p. 14.
19. *U.S. News & World Report,* Aug. 14, 1967, pp. 26-27; and Aug. 21, 1967, pp. 64-65.
20. *The New York Times,* Aug. 3, 1967.
21. *U.S. News & World Report,* Aug. 14, 1967, p. 26.
22. *The New York Times,* July 27, 1967.
23. *The New York Times,* July 28, 1967.
24. *The New York Times,* Aug. 7, 1967, p. 1.
25. AP Dispatch, Aug. 11, 1967.
26. *The New York Times,* Aug. 19, 1967.
27. *St. Louis Post-Dispatch,* Sept. 11, 1967.
28. *Alton Evening Telegraph,* Sept. 12, 1967, p. 1.
29. *Road to Revolution,* p. 55.
30. *St. Louis Post-Dispatch,* Aug. 16, 1967.
31. *Chicago Tribune,* Aug. 5, 1967.
32. *U.S. News & World Report,* Aug. 14, 1967, p. 23.
33. *The New York Times,* July 26, 1967.
34. *Chicago Tribune,* Aug. 6, 1967, p. 8.
35. *Chicago Tribune,* Aug. 12, 1967.
36. *Road to Revolution,* pp. 27-28.
37. *The New York Times,* Aug. 25, 1967.
38. *Road to Revolution,* p. 10.
39. Ibid., p. 11.
40. Ibid., pp. 117-121.
41. *U.S. News & World Report,* Aug. 14, 1967, p. 25.

IV. End of the Long, Hot Summer

1. *Chicago Tribune,* Sept. 7, 1967.
2. *New Politics News* (official NCNP publication), No. 1, p. 2.

3. *Chicago Tribune*, Sept. 2, 1967, p. 3.
4. *Chicago Daily News*, Sept. 1, 1967, p. 3.
5. *Chicago Tribune*, Sept. 5, 1967.
6. *The New York Times*, Sept. 4, 1967.
7. *The New York Times*, Sept. 3, 1967.
8. *St. Louis Post-Dispatch*, Sept. 3, 1967.
9. *The Liberal Papers* (Doubleday & Co., 1962), pp. 151-152.
10. *St. Louis Globe-Democrat*, Aug. 30, 1967. The Senate Internal Security Subcommittee later uncovered evidence that more than 75 Communist Party members participated as delegates, and the Party held key places on every committee and panel.
11. Ibid.
12. *Chicago Tribune*, Aug. 27, 1967, p. 24.
13. Schlafly and Ward, *Strike From Space*, pp. 139-142.
14. American Security Council, *Washington Report*, Sept. 4, 1967.
15. Chesly Manly of the *Chicago Tribune*, Aug. 27, 1967, p. 24. Manly is the same reporter who in July 1967 scooped the world's press, as well as the State Department, by obtaining the exact texts of the proposed three Panama Canal treaties and having them published in his newspaper.
16. Voting at the Convention was by a complex weighted formula by which each delegate theoretically cast one vote for every active worker he represented.
17. *Washington Post* News Service, Sept. 4, 1967.
18. *The New York Times*, Sept. 3, 1967, p. 4E.
19. *St. Louis Post-Dispatch*, Sept. 2, 1967, pp. 1ff.
20. *The New York Times*, Sept. 1, 1967.
21. *Chicago Tribune*, Sept. 3, 1967, p. 10.

V. Leadership: Cringing or Courageous?

1. It is interesting that *The New York Times* and many other newspapers shielded Rockefeller by not printing this story.
2. *U.S. News & World Report*, Oct. 2, 1967, p. 84.
3. *The New York Times*, Aug 8, 1967; *U.S. News & World Report*, Aug. 14, 1967, p. 40.
4. *U.S. News & World Report*, Aug. 14, 1967, pp. 40-42.
5. NANA Syndicated Column, Aug. 10, 1967.
6. *The New York Times*, July 26, 1967.
7. *U.S. News & World Report*, Aug. 14, 1967, p. 27.
8. *Chicago Tribune*, Aug. 14, 1967.
9. *U.S. News & World Report*, Aug. 21, 1967, p. 65.
10. NANA Syndicated Column, Aug. 1967. In this article Mr. Schuyler also gives startling statistics on how well off the American Negro is, and the fact that he has *twice* as good a chance of going to college as Europeans.

11. *Meet the Press,* July 16, 1967.
12. *U.S. News & World Report,* Nov. 30, 1964, p. 56. For background on King, see generally, Dr. James D. Bales, *The Martin Luther King Story,* 1967.
13. *Chicago Tribune,* Aug. 16 & Aug. 17, 1967.
14. AP Dispatch, Aug. 10, 1967.
15. *San Diego Union,* Aug. 8, 1967.
16. *U.S. News & World Report,* Aug. 14, 1967, p. 27.
17. Ibid.
18. *U.S. News & World Report,* Aug. 21, 1967, p. 66.
19. *U.S. News & World Report,* Aug. 21, 1967, p. 64.
20. *Time,* Aug. 4, 1967.
21. *Chicago Tribune* Press Service, Aug. 12, 1967.
22. *Los Angeles Herald Examiner,* Aug. 23, 1967.
23. *St. Louis Globe-Democrat,* July 1-2, 1967, p. 4F.
24. Edith Kermit Roosevelt, Syndicated Column, June 1967.
25. *U.S. News & World Report,* Aug. 23, 1965, p. 54.
26. *U.S. News & World Report,* Feb. 17, 1964, p. 16.
27. *St. Louis Post-Dispatch,* Aug. 16, 1967.
28. *U.S. News & World Report,* Aug. 14, 1967, p. 27.
29. *Detroit Free Press,* Aug. 20, 1967.
30. *U.S. News & World Report,* Sept. 11, 1967, p. 41.
31. *U.S. News & World Report,* Aug. 28, 1967, p. 52.
32. *Saturday Evening Post,* Sept. 9, 1967, p. 14.
33. *U.S. News & World Report,* Sept. 4, 1967, pp. 50-53.
34. Allen-Scott Report, Syndicated Column, Sept. 1967.
35. *Chicago Tribune,* Sept. 3, 1967.
36. *The New York Times,* July 8, 1967.
37. *Mallory v. U.S.* (354 U.S. 449, 1957) set aside a conviction for rape because the Washington police questioned Mallory for 8 hours (with pauses for rest and food) and obtained 3 voluntary confessions before calling a Commissioner to enter his plea and fix his bail. *Escobedo v. Illinois* (378 U.S. 478, 1964) set aside a conviction of murder based on a voluntary confession because the accused was not permitted to talk to his lawyer until after his interrogation. (Escobedo was arrested Sept. 22, 1967 as a member of a narcotics ring.) *Preston v. U.S.* (376 U.S. 364, 1964) set aside a conviction of conspiracy to rob a bank. The police had arrested 3 vagrants at 3 AM and, in searching their car, found 2 loaded revolvers, face masks, and an illegal license plate equipped to be snapped over another plate. One of the men then confessed they were preparing to rob a bank. The Court said the police violated the Constitution by searching their car. *Miranda v. Arizona* (384 U.S. 436, 1966) set aside a conviction for kidnapping and rape based on Miranda's voluntary con-

fession "made with full knowledge of my legal rights" because the police did not provide a lawyer for him during his interrogation.

38. *St. Louis Globe-Democrat,* July 1-2, 1967, p. 4F.
39. *U.S. News & World Report,* Aug. 28, 1967, p. 52.
40. *The New York Times,* Aug. 31, 1967.
41. *St. Louis Post-Dispatch,* Sept. 3, 1967.
42. Survey by Dr. Nathan Cohan for the University of California at Los Angeles, reported in *U.S. News & World Report,* Sept. 11, 1967.
43. *The New York Times,* Sept. 27, 1967.
44. According to Police Chiefs John B. Layton of Washington, D.C. and Thomas Reddin of Los Angeles, California.
45. *FBI Law Enforcement Bulletin,* Vol. 34, No. 1, Jan., 1965.
46. Speech by New York policeman Robert B. Walsh on the Manion Forum, Aug. 20, 1967.
47. June 13, 1961, pp. 2-3.
48. Speech entitled "The Causes and the Effects Upon Public Order of Planned, Mass Violation of Our Laws," Washington, D.C., Feb. 1967.
49. *U.S. News & World Report,* Sept. 18, 1967, p. 53.

VI. TFX: The Flying Edsel

1. Reprinted in Clark R. Mollenhoff, *Despoilers of Democracy,* 1965, pp. 399-402.
2. U.S. Senate Government Operations Committee, Permanent Subcommittee on Investigations, Hearings on the TFX Contract, 1963, Part 3, p. 726.
3. TFX Hearings, Part 2, p. 523.
4. *Congressional Record,* July 2, 1964, p. 15383.
5. TFX Hearings, Part 3, p. 768.
6. The Soviet air show at Domodedovo Airport in July 1967 featured new Mikoyan variable sweep-wing fighters and new Sukhoi variable sweep-wing attack planes.
7. Statement of Senator John McClellan, March 13, 1963.
8. *Congressional Record,* July 2, 1964, p. 15383.
9. *Saturday Evening Post,* June 17, 1967, p. 39.
10. TFX Hearings, Part 3, p. 699.
11. TFX Hearings, Part 3, p. 792, 799.
12. *Saturday Evening Post,* June 17, 1967, p. 39.
13. Reprinted in *Despoilers of Democracy,* pp. 405-411.
14. *The New York Times,* May 23, 1963.
15. TFX Hearings, Part 3, p. 883.
16. *Despoilers of Democracy,* p. 191.
17. *Saturday Evening Post,* June 17, 1966, p. 40.
18. *St. Louis Globe-Democrat,* Sept. 16-17, 1967.
19. *Saturday Evening Post,* June 17, 1967, p. 42.

20. Ibid.
21. Hearing held on July 14, 1967, released Sept. 13, 1967 and reported in *U.S. News & World Report,* Sept. 24, 1967, pp. 78-79.
22. It lacks maneuverability. The Air Force wanted the Boeing design because its thrust reversers made "for increased maneuverability." See McNamara "Memorandum" of Nov. 21, 1962 cited above.
23. Admiral David L. McDonald, Chief of Naval Operations, testified that recent studies concluded that even when the FB-111 becomes operational, the Navy "also would have to have another fighter plane aboard the carrier. Now when we came to that conclusion it eased the minds of a hell of a lot of people." AP Dispatch, Sept. 14, 1967.
24. The distance the Air Force F-111 can travel at supersonic speed on a low-level bomb run has been reduced by 75% from that expected. The intercontinental-ferry range is about 1,000 miles short of that originally planned.
25. This problem is due in part to the air inlet ducts under the wing roots. General Dynamics had copied the Boeing swing wing and high-lift devices but neglected to copy the Boeing top-mounted engine air inlet ducts. See Blackburn "Memorandum" cited above.
26. AP Dispatch, Aug. 12, 1967.
27. *Louisville Courier-Journal,* Sept. 18, 1966.

VII. The Big Payoff

1. *Congressional Record,* July 2, 1964, p. 15384.
2. Clark R. Mollenhoff, *Despoilers of Democracy,* 1965, pp. 151-152.
3. *Fort Worth Star-Telegram,* Dec. 12, 1962, p. 1.
4. *St. Louis Post-Dispatch,* Oct. 3, 1963, p. 2A; Oct. 31, 1963, p. 1; Dec. 10, 1963, p. 8A. Indictment and Judgment in *U.S. v. Erwin B. Arvey,* No. 63Cr 270(1), St. Louis Federal Court.
5. *St. Louis Post-Dispatch,* Jan. 21, 1964; Sept. 14, 1964, p. 8C; Sept. 15, 1964.
6. *Life* Magazine, May 26, 1967, p. 76B.
7. *St. Louis Post-Dispatch,* Dec. 22, 1963, p. 2A.
8. *Chicago Tribune,* July 14, 1967.
9. *Life* Magazine, Sept. 8, 1967, p. 103.
10. Ibid.
11. Arthur Bliss Lane, *I Saw Poland Betrayed,* 1946, p. 237.
12. U.S. Senate Foreign Relations Committee, Hearings on Nomination of Dean Acheson as Secretary of State, Jan. 13, 1949, pp. 2-6.
13. TFX Hearings, Part 4, pp. 1092-1093.

14. TFX Hearings, Part 7, p. 1883.
15. U.S. Senate Armed Services Committee, Hearings on the Korth Nomination, Jan. 18, 1962, p. 4.
16. *Congressional Record,* July 28, 1964, pp. 19768-19770.
17. *The New York Times,* Sept. 1, 1967, p. 12.
18. Speech of Senator Peter Dominick, *Congressional Record,* Sept. 19, 1967.
19. *Chicago Tribune,* Sept. 23, 1967.
20. *Chicago Tribune,* Sept. 25, 1967.
21. *The New York Times,* Sept. 15, 1967.

VIII. The Injustice Department

1. 364 U.S. 520, 1961.
2. Title 18, U.S. Code #208.
3. *Congressional Record,* July 18, 1963, p. 12585.
4. Ordered by U.S. District Judge Claude F. Clayton at Oxford, Mississippi.
5. AP Dispatch from Santa Barbara, California, Aug. 24, 1967.
6. Phillip Abbott Luce, *Road to Revolution,* 1967, p. 99.
7. Letter to *Human Events,* Sept. 23, 1967.
8. July 30, 1967, p. 3.
9. *Yates v. United States,* 354 U.S. 298, 1957.
10. Sept. 9-10, 1967, p. 2F.
11. Congressional Record, Sept. 11, 1967.
12. *St. Louis Post-Dispatch,* Sept. 3, 1967.
13. *St. Louis Globe-Democrat,* Sept. 27, 1967, p. 16A; David Lawrence Syndicated Column, Sept. 29, 1967.
14. June 26, 1967, p. 1.
15. *U.S. Code,* Title 39, #4006; Title 18, #1461.
16. *Ginzburg v. U.S.,* 383 U.S. 463, 466, 471.
17. *Eugene Dennis, et al. v. U.S.,* 341 U.S. 494, 509.
18. Statement before the Senate Internal Security Subcommittee.

IX. Leadership: Corrupt or Moral?

1. Lee Meriwether, *Jim Reed: Senatorial Immortal,* 1948.
2. *Congressional Record,* Sept. 22, 1950, p. 1950.
3. Martin Dies, *Martin Dies' Story,* 1963.
4. *U.S. News & World Report,* Feb. 6, 1967, p. 8.
5. *China Post,* Aug. 11, 1967, p. 4.
6. Details given by Jack Brooks in the *Vancouver Sun,* July 8, 1965; and by *St. Louis Post-Dispatch* reporter James Deakin in "The Dark Side of LBJ," *Esquire,* Aug. 1967.
7. *U.S. News & World Report,* June 12, 1967, p. 14.
8. *Los Angeles Times* News Service, Oct. 18, 1966.

9. *Despoilers of Democracy*, pp. 296-298, 310-313.
10. *Clive Boutilier v. Immigration and Naturalization Service*, 18 L ed 2d 661, 669.

X. Why Don't We Win In Vietnam?

1. For example, Marine Lieutenant General Lewis M. Walt, commander of U.S. troops in the First Corps area just south of the demilitarized zone, told the Veterans of Foreign Wars Convention in New Orleans on August 25, 1967 that victory might take 15 years. AP Dispatch.
2. According to Senator Stuart Symington, *St. Louis Globe-Democrat*, Jan. 27, 1967. Symington read to the Senate a number of statements given him in Vietnam by American airmen. One pilot said: "I fly over barges that have been unloaded from ships and see on their decks the trucks, ammunition, and oil which later I attack with questionable success in the jungles of the Ho Chi Minh trails. Is not a North Vietnamese barge loaded with weapons and ammunition a legitimate target?"
3. Speech in Detroit, Dec. 6, 1965.
4. AP Dispatch, London, June 16, 1967.
5. *St. Louis Globe-Democrat*, Sept. 16, 1967.
6. *U.S. News & World Report*, Oct. 2, 1967, p. 22.
7. *The New York Times*, Sept. 1, 1967, p. 1.
8. *U.S. News & World Report*, Aug. 28, 1967, p. 8.
9. *Newsweek*, Sept. 12, 1966, p. 22.
10. *The New York Times*, Aug. 26, 1967, p. 4.
11. Pages 26-28.
12. The reason for the big spread of the lines showing U.S. and U.S.S.R. deliverable megatonnage is that the exact figures are classified and cannot be revealed. Many of the men who signed the Schriever Report have had access to classified information on nuclear weapons. In order for them not to be charged with improper disclosure of classified information, the Big X Chart was made up solely from *un*classified sources, which are subject to some variation because of different methods of figuring megatonnage. However, we have the word of the 17 distinguished men on the Schriever Committee that the accurate figures are somewhere within the spread. The important part of the Big X Chart is that U.S. *superiority* to the Soviets in 1962 changed to U.S. *inferiority* to the Soviets in 1967. On this unhappy comparison all authorities agree, no matter how they figure the power of specific weapons systems.
13. Here is how McNamara has scrapped half our megatonnage delivery capability. He scrapped ¾ of our strategic bombers, and has announced plans for scrapping ⅔ of

those still remaining. He scrapped ¾ of our *multi*-megaton intercontinental ballistic missiles, and has announced plans for scrapping all those remaining. He scrapped all our intermediate and medium-range ballistic missiles, and abandoned our bases near the Soviet Union from which they could be used. Meanwhile, the Soviets have their base in Cuba, and many believe their missiles are still there. He has refused to build the Nike X anti-missile (unanimously recommended by the Joint Chiefs of Staff) to protect us from the Soviets, even though they are deploying their anti-missile system. He has refused to allow the U.S. to build space weapons even though the Soviets have displayed their 30-megaton orbital weapon, the Scrag.

14. U.S. Senate Foreign Relations Committee, Hearings on the Nuclear Test Ban Treaty, Aug. 13, 1963, p. 100.

XI. Leadership: For Surrender or for Freedom?

1. *Chicago Tribune*, July 9, 1967.
2. In addition to the weapons and aircraft scrapped which were listed in footnote 13 of Chapter 10, McNamara has cancelled all *new* weapons systems including Skybolt, Pluto, Dynasoar, and Orion, as well as the B-70 or any advanced manned strategic aircraft.
3. *Chicago Tribune*, July 26, 1967.
4. *The New York Times*, Sept. 15, 1967.
5. The value of the Nike X Anti-Missile is explained in Schlafly and Ward, *Strike from Space*, especially Chapter 21.
6. According to briefs filed in the Civil Service case of Otto F. Otepka, chief security evaluator for the State Department, and reported in the *St. Louis Globe-Democrat*, Oct. 4, 1967, p. 1.
7. *Congressional Quarterly Weekly Report*, Jan. 21, 1966, p. 68.
8. *Chicago Tribune*, June 22, 1967, p. 1.
9. *The New York Times*, May 26, 1967.
10. When Khrushchev came to the U.S. in 1959, he visited with Cyrus Eaton and gave him a valuable troika complete with matched horses. Kosygin also visited Eaton after the Glassboro meeting with LBJ.
11. Speech in Honolulu, *Honolulu Advertiser*, July 2, 1967.

XII. The Purge

1. *Los Angeles Times*, July 2, 1965.
2. *Tampa Tribune*, July 29, 1965.
3. *Detroit Free Press*, Sept. 4, 1965.

4. Schlafly & Ward, *The Gravediggers,* pp. 115-116.
5. *Long Beach Independent,* May 14, 1965, p. 1.
6. *Long Beach Press-Telegram,* Mar. 8, 1967.
7. In a press conference in Washington, D.C., May 2, 1967, and in an open letter of June 6, 1967.
8. At a meeting on Mar. 30, 1965 in Washington, D.C.
9. *St. Louis Post-Dispatch,* Jan. 19, 1967, p. 6A.
10. *Alton Telegraph,* Jan. 24, 1967, p. 1.
11. *Alton Telegraph,* Jan. 25, 1967.
12. *Chicago Tribune,* Jan. 26, 1967. So far as I know, this was the only newspaper account printed anywhere concerning the actual election of the Nominating Committee on Jan. 25, 1967.
13. Letter of Jan. 27, 1967 on NFRW letterhead.
14. Interview with Mrs. Ruth Parks in the *Denver Post,* Feb. 6, 1967.
15. These included the "cockroach" story described later, releases on the Goldwater letter described later, and also the leaking of the official club list to Mrs. O'Donnell sometime earlier than it was mailed to Mrs. Schlafly, in complete violation of fair play.
16. *Washington Star,* Mar. 23, 1967.
17. *St. Louis Post-Dispatch,* Apr. 6, 1967.
18. *Tulsa Tribune,* June 30, 1967.
19. Article III, Sect. 4, and Article VIII, Sect. 2(c).
20. *Los Angeles Times,* June 30, 1967.
21. Syndicated Column, May 17, 1967.
22. Letter of June 6, 1967.
23. AP Dispatch, May 4, 1967. Typical headlines read: "Mrs. Schlafly's Guards Will Watch Guards."
24. Article VI, Sec. 2(b).
25. June 20, 1967.
26. Telegram, May 8, 1967.
27. *Columbus Dispatch,* May 14, 1967.

XIII. Don't Leave Politics to the Politicians

1. American Conservative Union, *The D.M.V. Report,* 1967.
2. Here are some suggestions for starting your study: "Lets Make This an Honest Election!", *Reader's Digest,* Sept. 1964, p. 53. "How to Steal an Election," *Changing Times,* Oct. 1966, p. 45. W. H. Cooper, *What You Should Know About Rigging Voting Machines* (3176 Alaska St., Baton Rouge, La.). "Operation Eagle Eye," *National Review,* Nov. 3, 1964, p. 941. Speech of Paul Findley, *Congressional Record,* Oct. 2, 1964, p. A5082.

About the Author—

Phyllis Schlafly has been on the inside of Republican politics since 1952, and is now First Vice President of the National Federation of Republican Women. She is best known as the author of A CHOICE NOT AN ECHO which, without a single advertisement, sold three million copies in 1964.

She is also the co-author, with Rear Admiral Chester Ward, USN (Ret.), of two best-selling books on our nuclear defense: THE GRAVEDIGGERS (1964) and STRIKE FROM SPACE (first edition, 1965; second edition, 1966). From 1962 to 1966 Mrs. Schlafly conducted a weekly radio program called AMERICA WAKE UP, a commentary on national and international affairs, heard on 25 stations.

Mrs. Schlafly has held *elective* positions on every level of political action—precinct, district, state, and national—and has received many awards for dedicated *volunteer* service. She was elected Delegate to the Republican National Convention in 1956, 1960 (Alternate), and 1964.

Phyllis Schlafly worked her way through college, graduated with honors from Washington University in St. Louis, and received a Master's Degree from Radcliffe College, Cambridge, Massachusetts, specializing in Government. She is a member of Phi Beta Kappa and Pi Sigma Alpha (the Political Science honorary).

She is the mother of six children and the wife of Fred Schlafly. They live on a bluff overlooking the Mississippi River at Alton, Illinois.

In naming her "Woman of Achievement in Public Affairs" in 1963, the *St. Louis Globe-Democrat* said: "Phyllis Schlafly stands for everything that has made America great and for those things which will keep it that way."

Other Best-Sellers by Phyllis Schlafly

STRIKE FROM SPACE

with Rear Admiral Chester Ward, USN (Ret.) How LBJ and McNamara are disarming America while the Soviets prepare to attack.

A CHOICE NOT AN ECHO

what the New York kingmakers have done to the Republican Party
———— 3 million copies sold ————

THE GRAVEDIGGERS

with Rear Admiral Chester Ward, USN (Ret.) How White House secret advisers are digging our graves

----

PERE MARQUETTE PRESS
P. O. Box 495, Alton, Illinois 62002

Send_____copies SAFE—NOT SORRY

_____copies STRIKE FROM SPACE

Single Copy: $1.00

3 copies: ,2.25	20 copies: $10.00
10 copies: 6.00	100 copies: 30.00

Send_____copies A CHOICE NOT AN ECHO

_____copies THE GRAVEDIGGERS

1 copy: $.75	10 copies: $5	100 copies: $30
3 copies: $2	25 copies: $10	500 copies: $125

Illinois residents add 4% sales tax

Name_____
(Please print)

Street_____

City_____ State_____ Zip_____

Do you want to pull your neighbor out of his easy chair and into the ranks of political action?

Then give **SAFE — NOT SORRY** the handbook on current political issues

To Friends and Neighbors, whether Republicans, Democrats or Independents. In politics there is no substitute for door-to-door precinct work.

Ask doctors to give this book to their patients, employers to their employees, parents to college and high school students. Give it to opinionmakers such as editors, radio and TV commentators, clergymen, teachers, writers, and elected officials. Give it to members of your church, club, union or fraternity. Distribute it at meetings, on trains, in motels.

POLITICS IS EVERYBODY'S BUSINESS!
PERE MARQUETTE PRESS

P. O. Box 495   Alton, Illinois 62002